The Teaching Assistant's Guide to Literacy

Also available from Continuum:

How to be a Successful Teaching Assistant – Jill Morgan
101 Essential Lists for Teaching Assistants – Louise Burnham
Teaching Assistant's Handbook: Primary Edition – Janet Kay

The Teaching Assistant's Guide to Literacy

Susan Elkin

continuum

Continuum International Publishing Group
The Tower Building   80 Maiden Lane
11 York Road   Suite 704
London, SE1 7NX   New York, NY 10038

www.continuumbooks.com

British Library Cataloguing-in-Publication Data
A catalogue record for this book is available from the British Library.

ISBN: 0–8264–9367–X (paperback)

Typeset by Kenneth Burnley, Wirral, Cheshire
Printed and bound in Great Britain by Ashford Colour Press,
Gosport, Hampshire

Contents

A bit of background

What do we mean by literacy?

The word 'literacy' is all around us. But it doesn't mean quite what it used to. Once literacy was something acquired by previously unschooled people. When, at last, they found themselves in classrooms they learned to decipher squiggles on paper and became literate – perhaps in Victorian Britain or colonial Africa.

Now it is a school subject, parts of which would once have been called 'English'. And it is often used as a describing word or adjective in, for example, 'literacy teaching' or 'literacy hour'. Primary teachers, in particular, now talk of literacy – rather than English – lessons. Pupils use it in this way too. The word also tends to get borrowed these days for use in other contexts. People speak of 'emotional literacy' or 'computer literacy'.

Collins English Dictionary defines literacy simply as 'the ability to read and write' or, secondly, as 'the ability to use language proficiently'. That seems straightforward, but actually it isn't. Does the ability to read mean just being able to work out single words like danger or ladies? Or does it mean that you can read and effortlessly understand a newspaper like *The Times* or the latest Harry Potter book? Or does it mean something in between? 'Proficiently' is somewhat vague.

In fact, becoming literate is not an event in a child's life like having an eighth birthday or breaking an arm. It's a process. It starts at birth and it continues for the whole of life. Literacy acquisition does not stop at the end of school or childhood. We all go on becoming more literate as we read more, learn more words and practise using language in all sorts of ways.

The secret – for those working with children – is to manage the process and to make sure it gets off to a fine start. We have to see that every child gets all the help and support he or she needs to become a proficient language user. And that's where you, the teaching assistant – often called a learning assistant because you assist children's learning – have a big part to play.

Sometimes, for various reasons, children don't make the progress with literacy development that they should, so they fall behind. Over 20 per cent of 11-year-olds leaving primary school do not read and write at the level now regarded as a minimum. These children in particular need urgent help from teaching assistants – and others – when they start secondary school.

No one is born literate. It has to be learned.

 Think about how you learnt to read. Who taught you? What did you find easiest or most difficult? Reflecting on this will help you to understand what the children are experiencing.

Aspects of literacy

Literacy education has four strands:

- listening
- speaking
- reading
- writing.

Before we can read and write we have to speak and listen. That is why babies need to hear voices and words. Parents and other carers of young children have a responsibility to expose them to language. This is the beginning of literacy.

For a long time a child will not be able to read a word or use it herself if she hasn't, at some time, heard someone else use it. The more words a child hears – the larger her vocabulary – the more readily she becomes literate. So children who come from homes where adults do not speak to, sing to or play with babies and toddlers or who have not had good nursery education will already be disadvantaged when they start school. All adults at the school are involved in helping the child to catch up.

The sounds babies make are the beginning of speech. That is why they must be encouraged. It is also why, years later, teachers encourage pupils to talk. Using the spoken word, and responding to what others say, is an important part of literacy development.

Chapter 2 of this book looks at what comes before reading and writing in more detail, with some ideas for how to build on it in school.

Reading comes before writing, but children need to be encouraged to write from the beginning. Drawing is a stepping stone on the way to writing because the child is learning to put meaning on paper, and also how to manage pencils, crayons and brushes. Once children get to the age of three or four they often do 'pretend' writing and tell adults what it 'says'. This is a clear sign that they are beginning to understand what writing is for.

Handwriting is part of literacy. So too, eventually, is learning to use a keyboard – ideally using ten-finger touch-typing because it's fast and efficient.

There are many ways of working on listening, speaking, reading and writing other than working from books, although, of course, books are a very important part of literacy work. For example, drama activities – make-believe play for the youngest children – are a good way of developing children's use of language.

The National Curriculum and the National Strategies

The National Curriculum is a framework. It sets down what every state school pupil, aged 5–16, should learn in every subject. It was introduced in the 1980s and has been changed and adapted many times since.

Children take written National Curriculum tests in English, mathematics and science at the end of Year 2, Year 6 and Year 9. These are also known as End of Key Stage Tests, or SATs (Standard Assessment Tests). Candidates have to read the test papers and write their answers, so literacy skills affect the science and mathematics tests as well as the English ones. The tests are assessed at eight levels, and the Government wants as many people as possible to achieve minimum levels, as the chart below shows.

Minimum National Curriculum levels

Age	School year	Key Stage	Expected NC level
6/7	2	1	2
10/11	6	2	4
13/14	9	3	5

Some children – often picked out as being 'gifted and talented' and in need of activities to extend them – achieve well above the minimum levels. You may find yourself working with small groups of these pupils too.

In the late 1990s the Government decided that the National Curriculum was not doing enough to develop literacy. So, in 1998, it introduced the National Literacy Strategy (and a parallel National Numeracy Strategy).

This brought the literacy hour for primary schools. Every state school was expected to spend an hour a day for 5–11-year-olds specifically on literacy. The recommended pattern for the hour was 15 minutes explaining the topic followed by

15 minutes of whole-class work on words or sentences. Then the children worked in groups or individually for 20 minutes. The typical hour ended with a ten-minute 'plenary' or review session in which the children answered questions to remind themselves of what they'd learned. The content of the literacy hour was laid out quite rigidly week by week and term by term.

The National Literacy Strategy has now been absorbed by the broader Primary National Strategy. The literacy hour is still taught, but it's more flexible than it used to be and it now includes speaking and listening work.

Then the Government turned its attention to 11–14-year-olds in secondary schools. Too many were arriving in Year 7 without having reached level 4. Even more worrying, others, who had achieved level 4, were slipping backwards during Years 7 and 8. These problems tend to affect boys more than girls, but there were problems with both sexes.

The Key Stage 3 Strategy – which in 2003 became part of the Secondary National Strategy – arrived in the school year 2000/1. Its aim is to help pupils who come into Year 7 at below level 4 make faster progress and to help other groups of pupils who need additional support.

The Secondary National Strategy is the main reason why so many more teaching assistants are employed in secondary schools than used to be. If you are one of these you will spend a great deal of your time helping individual pupils within lessons. Under the guidance of a teacher you might also do small group work with pupils who need extra support.

The two strategies together have changed the way that primary and secondary classes are taught. It now tends to be a team effort and you are an important team member. The teacher leads one or more teaching assistants, rather than running the class alone.

 Think about literacy teaching today compared with in the past. Do you think children are taught literacy more systematically now than you were when you were at school or, perhaps, when your own children were at school?

Literacy across the curriculum

Every school subject involves words, and most require some reading and writing. Anything that a pupil does at school requires some listening.

For example, when you study geometry in mathematics you learn new words such as isosceles, parallelogram, rhombus and sphere. Some of these have tricky spellings and they need to be learned too. Using the vocabulary accurately is half way to understanding the concepts. As TA you can help with this.

A Year 5 class in PE has to listen to the teacher – and possibly the teaching assistant – giving instructions. He or she might also be telling the class how better to catch a ball or tackle an opponent in a team game. And there will be safety reminders and rules such as, 'Don't throw the ball until you hear the whistle.'

A pupil in Year 8 who is studying the French Impressionists in art, and experimenting with their styles, will also need to read about these artists – in reference books or on the Internet. The teacher will probably ask for written notes too.

Most resources for citizenship or PSHE (personal, social and health education) – at all ages – include some writing, even if it's only a label on a diagram.

It might help you to think of other examples of how literacy applies to subjects other than English. What about history, geography, music, RE and science, for example?

Catching up

The child who falls behind in literacy will fall behind in everything else too. You will probably find yourself working particularly with children in primary school who didn't achieve level 2 at the end of Key Stage 2 and in secondaries with those who didn't get to level 4 before they finished primary school. These are the children who have fallen behind and need help to catch up. TAs are likely frontline providers of that help.

These children are already behind their age group. They need help. But they may not welcome it. It isn't usually a good idea to offer them a repeat of what didn't work for them the first time round. We have to think of something else – and there are practical ideas for that in this book.

One problem is that of the pupil – typically a boy – who arrives in Year 8 still at, say, level 2. He has been failing for some years so he's pretty turned off school – the sort that educationists and teachers call 'disaffected'. He's now a brawny adolescent and will not want to be made to look at the 'baby' books used for children at level 2 who are five or six years younger. The challenge in catch-up literacy work is to find reading material which is at the right reading level but with content to catch his interest.

In short, we live in a written world and children need the best possible levels of literacy to access it, both at school and elsewhere. So let's now look at the practicalities.

Before literacy

This chapter is about working with children of all ages who have not yet acquired print literacy. It deals with ways of helping pupils *towards* reading and writing rather than helping them to learn the formal literacy skills which we look at in Chapters 3 and 4.

Foundation Stage and Key Stage 1

Most children in the UK begin to recognize letters and word shapes between the ages of three and five. A few are more advanced and will be reading whole sentences or books at this early stage. Others are not yet ready to connect marks on paper with meaning linked to the sounds they hear all around them.

That is why the youngest children in school need as many word-related activities as possible. It helps those who didn't get this stimulation at home or elsewhere before they started school. It speeds up English language acquisition in children from homes where English is not spoken, perhaps because the family is newly arrived in Britain. And it further develops word awareness in all children.

As a classroom assistant – or nursery nurse in the case of the youngest children – who is aware of the need to engage in these word-play activities, you can do a lot to help build them into the everyday lives of the children you work with.

Drawing and making patterns

A baby of nine months sitting in a high chair makes scrubbing marks on a piece of paper with a crayon. That is the beginning of the process of learning to write.

Typically such infants make circles first then, in time, they will say that the circle is someone's face – with dots for the eyes and mouth. Later they add arms and legs (usually not noticing the existence of a body). Gradually it gets more detailed. Then, because they see adults writing, eventually they pretend to write because they know that writing means something and that grown-ups can read it. At that stage art – drawing, painting and so on – gets a separate life of its own as part of what the child likes to do.

Sadly, not all children are given the opportunity to draw and 'write' before they start school, and the ones that are well grounded need to go on progressing. So once they're in school all children need lots of encouragement to make marks on paper at their own level. That means:

- drawing with pencils, coloured pencils, crayons, felt tips, etc.
- painting – with brushes or fingers
- making repeat patterns with, for example, cut carrot ends dipped in paint
- making hand and foot print patterns
- doing any other art work that teachers and teaching assist-ants can organize.

As they get better at controlling pencils, pens and crayons, children can be encouraged to make patterns involving lines which, like English writing, start on the left of the paper and continue to the right – straight, curly, zigzag or anything else they wish. Then they can colour the pattern.

Before he or she can become literate a child has to learn that written English starts in the top left-hand corner of a page. It then moves in lines across the page from left to right. (Other languages such as Arabic or Chinese are written quite differently.) Making patterns based on this trains the eye for later reading. It is also a way of beginning to get the hand used to moving in the right direction for later writing.

Singing

Singing activities help children to get used to the rhythms of language. They also get them to speak words and make the children more confident with language. It is an important pre-literacy activity. Sing with the children you work with every day. Don't worry if you think you don't have much of a singing voice. The children are not music critics. Do it with confidence and they will join in happily.

Remember that very young children find it difficult to sing very high or low notes, so stick to songs which don't move about much in pitch. Try traditional songs such as:

- 'Old Macdonald had a farm'
- 'One man went to mow'
- 'Wind the bobbin up'
- 'She'll be coming round the mountain'
- 'The wheels on the bus'
- 'If you're happy and you know it'.

Doing actions as you sing makes it more fun. And don't be afraid to make up new actions of your own.

Then there are moving-about singing games such as:

- 'The farmer's in his den'
- 'Poor Jenny is a-weeping'
- 'The big ship sailed'
- 'Head, shoulders, knees and toes'
- 'The hokey cokey'
- 'Here we go round the mulberry bush'.

Some songs help children to learn to take away or subtract numbers:

- 'There were ten in the bed'
- 'Once I caught a fish alive'
- 'Ten green bottles'.

You may want some religious song, and carols:

- 'Kum by ya'
- 'We will rock you'
- 'Mary had a baby, yes Lord'
- 'The ink is black'.

There are literally thousands of suitable songs to sing with children at this stage. Use CDs to learn new ones. You can, of course, put a CD on in the classroom and sing along with it if you like. But be careful not to drown out the children's voices. Find good CDs of children's songs via Internet shops where you can often listen to a sample via the computer. Or visit a large record shop which has a good selection. Here are a few suggestions:

- *Big Rock Candy Mountain: 23 songs for children* Sung by Burl Ives and others, Half Moon (1998)
- *100 Songs for Children*, Little Demon (2006)
- *Children's Favourites*, Platinum (2003)
- *Hymns and Songs for Children*, Spectrum (2006)
- *Five Little Frogs*, Playsongs Publications.

The good thing about singing is that you can do it anywhere. Of course, you might be sitting with a group of children having a sing-along, but you can also sing with children:

- while you're waiting with a child for another to come out of the toilet

- in a dinner or snack queue
- outside during breaks
- in minibuses, coaches or cars during visits away from school
- in any odd few minutes, when a task is finished but there's three minutes to go before playtime
- while doing jobs.

You can also adapt songs to fit what you're doing. If you are, say, taking two children to the school library you could sing as you go:

> Twinkle, twinkle little book
> How I wonder where to look
> Sitting on the library shelf
> Waiting quietly by itself
> Twinkle, twinkle little book
> How I wonder where to look.

Linda Caroe, a Welsh music and education adviser, has invented a tidying up song to the tune of 'The farmer's in his den':

> It's time to tidy up
> It's time to tidy up
> Ee i tiddley i
> It's time to tidy up.
> We're tidying up the floor
> We're tidying up the books . . .

It's also fun – and quite easy – to sing ordinary instructions to tunes the children know. Try singing to the tune of Frère Jacques:

> Come and sit down (*twice*)
> On the floor (*twice*)
> Sit quite close together (*twice*)
> In a group (*twice*).

Or you could try 'Wash your hands with lots of soap' to the first line of 'Baa, Baa Black Sheep'. The children will enjoy making these up with you.

Build singing into your activities as often as possible. A child with a speech impediment – a stammer, for example – can often sing perfectly fluently. That is why speech therapists often use singing as part of their programmes. It may, in time, help to correct the impediment and it will certainly build up the child's self-esteem, because this is something he or she can do as well as anyone else in the group.

Rhymes and stories

Many of today's children are not used to listening to words. In the past many children heard stories. Today nearly half of British four-year-olds have TVs in their bedrooms. Most stories on TV are visual and the child can understand without listening closely. That is partly why many young children arrive at school unable to listen well. They have had little practice.

But literacy depends on listening. You have to hear a word – on someone else's lips and/or in your own head – before you can read or write it. Stories and rhymes therefore matter very much in teaching literacy and preparing for it.

Another important function of stories and rhymes is that they build up vocabulary. They also develop children's imagination so that they can, in time, use language to make up their own stories or rhymes, written or spoken, or both. And probably most important of all, stories and rhymes are fun. Children (and teaching assistants and teachers!) enjoy them.

So any teacher that you work with, or school that you work in, will be looking for ways of exposing children to as many stories and rhymes as possible.

As a teaching assistant you might:

- tell or read a story to an individual child or small group
- use a puppet to tell a story

- tell the children about something which has happened to you, your family or your pet
- encourage the children to tell their own stories.

Useful resources for this include:

- things to show the children, such as photographs of your family and animals
- story cards which you can use to piece a story together – several publishers produce these
- story sacks – bags of items (for example, a baby's feeding bottle, an apple, a photograph of a woman, and dog's lead) around which you create a story
- story books to read aloud from
- large format story books so that the children can see the pictures
- puppets and soft toys
- hats so that you can pretend be an old lady, a pirate, a police officer or whatever.

There is a big difference between telling a story and reading one. If you tell a story from memory you have eye contact with the children. They are more likely to listen and engage with you than if you're reading. Listening to a story read aloud is a slightly more sophisticated skill, which children have to grow into.

Get the children to make up stories too. For example, you could have a teddy bear which becomes a little character in the lives of the group you are working with. Cover him with bandages. Ask the children what happened. Or make the bear shake because he is frightened. What's he scared of? Or he has gone on holiday. Where has he gone and what will he do?

There are many hundreds of books which very young children love sharing. You will have your own favourites and so will the children. Here are just a few possibilities. Like many books for pre-readers these all, in their different ways, have wonderful illustrations:

- *Jinnie Ghost* by Jane Ray and Berlie Doherty, Frances Lincoln Children's Books
- *Rosie's Walk* by Pat Hutchins, Red Fox
- *Lost and Found* by Oliver Jeffers, HarperCollins
- *Miffy* by Dick Bruna, Egmont Books
- *Russell the Sheep* by Rob Scotton, HarperCollins
- *10 Little Rubber Ducks* by Eric Carle, HarperCollins
- *The Big Sneeze* by Ruth Brown, Andersen Press

When you read aloud, point to the words as you go along. It shows the children what you're reading from and reminds them that written words carry meaning. The more advanced children will recognize some of the words you are pointing to.

Nursery rhymes and poems play with words in a rhythmic way. Like songs they help children to get used to the pleasure of fitting words together in a way which is fun. Some are spoken, many have tunes. Make sure that you know as many as possible – you will be able to recall several from your own childhood. And there are some very good books and CDs from which you can learn others that will probably be new to you.

Chant or sing them to the children – they will quickly learn to join in with you. Rhymes and poems are part of their national heritage, so it's a sad loss if children never experience them. They also have a key role to play in developing language fluency and getting children ready for formal literacy teaching.

Try these books and CDs for rhymes and poems to add to the ones you already know:

- *A Child's Treasury of Nursery Rhymes* (with CD) ed. Kady MacDonald Denton, Kingfisher
- *The Collins Book of Nursery Rhymes*, Collins
- *The Oxford Nursery Rhyme Book* by Iona and Peter Opie, Oxford University Press
- *Poems for Young Children* chosen by Philip Hawthorn, Usborne

■ *The Macmillan Treasury of Nursery Rhymes and Poems*, Macmillan Children's Books

■ *Sing a Song of Sixpence: Nursery Rhymes* (CD), Spectrum.

 Think about the reactions and behaviour of children you have used rhymes and songs with. What skills were they learning and what knowledge were they acquiring? How did it help your relationship with them?

Make-believe play

A lot of children's play depends on pretending: 'Let's pretend . . .' or 'Let's make believe . . .' Children will quite naturally invent situations based on their own experience and on stories they have been told. What they are actually doing is making up little plays – it's not a coincidence that we use the same word for what actors rehearse and put on in theatres.

Children will use any space that's available and any equipment, however primitive, that's around. So a cardboard box becomes a ship, a circle marked on the playground a house, a cardigan a wedding dress and so on. And all the time they are busy improvising their, often quite complicated, make-believe games, children are using language and developing their literacy, or working towards 'print literacy'.

That is why it is an important part of children's education and must be encouraged. The trouble is that, for the same reasons that many modern children find it difficult to listen, many no longer know how to play imaginatively. And adults too often fail to recognize how important it is, so they are constantly calling children away from play to make them do something else.

Give children time and space to play in and never dismiss it as something trivial which must be packed up so that you and the children can get on with 'something more important', like 'literacy'. Hang on tightly to the fact that make-believe play is part of developing literacy.

Many studies have involved researchers observing children

at play. See, for example, *The Excellence of Play* by Janet R. Moyles, published by Open University Press (2005). Observers usually comment on the quality of language work and the highly developed imaginativeness which children show if they are allowed and encouraged to play.

Classrooms are often planned to include play areas such as:

- a home corner (for playing mothers and fathers, cooking pretend meals, etc.)
- a dressing-up box (coloured garments to encourage games involving princesses, pirates, etc.)
- an empty space (for playing with complete freedom).

Items which encourage imaginative play include:

- old clothes (especially velvet, silk in different colours, handbags and hats)
- cardboard boxes
- scraps of fabric (in a range of colours and textures)
- small off-cuts of wood (smoothed off to avoid splinters)
- coloured paper (such as wallpaper leftovers)
- clean household waste (such as cardboard tubes, used gift wrap, etc.)
- ribbon.

You can encourage slightly more structured imaginative play by organizing the children into carefully thought-out play situations such as:

- at the hospital
- in the post office
- at the supermarket
- at the vets
- at the dentists
- in the park.

This is a good way to familiarize them with wider vocabulary which helps to move them towards literacy.

The class teacher may be concerned that some of the children in the class have too little experience of some situations to act them out. Early Vision produces some useful video and DVD theme packs to help get round this (www.earlyvision.co.uk).

As a teaching assistant you are likely to have the job of collecting and organizing resources for these sorts of activities. It is part of lesson preparation for which TAs help to reduce teacher workload.

 Observe some children playing a make-believe game. Don't interfere or try to help, just watch. Make notes and try to work out what the children are learning and how their literacy is benefiting.

After Key Stage 1

Most children reach Key Stage 1 with rapidly developing print literacy. But some, for various reasons, do not. They are still at the pre-literacy stage. Some are just 'late developers', just as some children walk and feed themselves later than others, so some learn to read later. We've all heard of children who don't read a word until they're ten years old and then go on to become university professors, but that's fairly unusual.

Either way, it means a gap between the pre-literate children and others in the class, and a challenging job for you to work with them. These children have to be encouraged and developed as positively as possible. The last thing anyone wants for them is that they begin to feel any sense of failure. Low self-esteem is very destructive and can, in itself, stop children progressing.

So the first general thing you can do is to take a lot of time and trouble with these children and give them every impression that you and other adults really care. More specifically from a pre-literacy point of view, these children need an older version of all the activities used at Key Stage 1, except that it must never seem babyish, or a repeat of something they did when they were younger.

Strategies could include:

■ Reading aloud and talking about stories. Look in the library for books which tell stories for the 7–11s. Most will now regard large format picture books as beneath them.

■ Chatting to the children and encouraging them to talk to you about the family, home, likes and dislikes, sport and anything else which engages them. Share your own thoughts too, so it's a proper conversation.

■ Role-play or make-believe play such as, 'Let's pretend you're selling stamps in the post office and I come to buy something from you.' Or, 'You be a cross mother and I'll be a child who has misbehaved', or 'You be the teacher and I'll be a Year 4 boy who needs help with something.' You can discuss, rehearse and develop it until the full situation is worked out.

As a teaching assistant you may sometimes be assigned to a specific child with special educational needs (SEN) or statement of SEN, although this is less common than it used to be.

After Key Stage 2

Even fewer children reach Key Stage 3 still at the pre-literate stage, but for the few who do the gap between them and nearly everyone else is now very wide. They are not young children, they are teenagers with teenage interests. There may be behaviour problems. Most will, by now, have been recognized as having learning difficulties, but a few will not have acquired print literacy for other reasons, such as:

- a history of illness and consequent lack of schooling (although there will have been other provision if the child was well enough)
- a background of school truancy, probably condoned by the family
- a nomadic life style, such as that experienced by some traveller children, where there are many changes of school and even some periods of no school
- many changes of school for some other reason, such as being in care
- recent arrival in the UK, with no previous education in English.

All children in the situations listed above – and the list is by no means exhaustive – have special educational needs (SEN). These needs, however, will not necessarily be detailed in a statement of special needs, a binding document issued by the local education authority which sets out, and promises, precisely the help a child needs after a detailed assessment.

Not all children with SEN have learning (or behavioural) difficulties, although all children with learning difficulties have special needs and it is important to understand the difference. For example:

Child 1 is a non-reading 12-year-old. He has learning difficulties caused by severe dyslexia. So he has SEN.

Child 2 is also 12 and she can't read at all either. She has attended eleven schools in four years and has lived in a succession of foster homes of varying quality. She has no discernible learning difficulty and is probably perfectly capable of becoming literate quite easily. But she has SEN partly because she's seriously behind and partly because she desperately needs stability.

You may be required to work with such pupils on an individually assigned basis or, more likely, your role will be to encourage them as part of the class or group with which you are working.

Remember:

- Pupils respond to adults showing interest. Treat them as sensible young adults and encourage them to talk. Build up trust. Every sentence they put together is another step towards print literacy.
- You are never too old to be read to. Find books at the right interest level and try to convince the pupil(s) that books are 'cool'.
- Role-play is not childish (it is often used in professional training for adults). As at Key Stage 2, use situations suitable for the pupils' age, for example, buying trainers, CDs or takeaway pizza, or enquiring about opening times at the swimming pool.

If your job means that you spend most of your time working with pupils who have fallen behind, think about how you can get their interest in literacy at the right level without patronizing them or 'putting them down'.

Working with children who have yet to learn English

Families arrive in the UK all the time from other countries. A few are asylum seekers. Most are immigrants who apply for, and are given, the chance to settle in Britain for a better life. Many of these children arrive in British schools with limited, or no, English. Remember that once they're at Key Stage 2, they probably have some print literacy in another language such as Bengali, but they are, until they have learned English, functionally illiterate in a British school.

All adults in a school need to be aware of how difficult that would be. Just imagine how you might feel if you were thrust into a work situation in, say, rural China where no one outside your own family could speak to you and where you understood not a word of the written language.

So, temporarily, it's another sort of special need. Most local education authorities (LEAs) – and schools where there are large numbers of children in need of English as a foreign language (EFL) support – offer such children special teaching. But they also have to settle in their schools and integrate with other pupils as they acquire literacy in the new language. You, as a TA, can do a lot to help.

The usual smiles and chats go a long way, and so do stories with plenty of pictures so that meaning is clear. Depending how the school or teacher organizes it, you may also be required to help the children with follow-up work after their specialist lessons.

Doing the job

Carol Pemberton is a teaching assistant at Barn Croft Primary School, Walthamstow. The school is in the Waltham Forest Education Authority but is run by Edu-Action, a private company. Carol has two children of her own, aged nine and seven, who attend a different school.

I first came here in 2003, having worked for a long time as a child minder. I have a National Nursery Examining Board (NNEB) qualification. My job description was simply 'to assist the teacher.' I was in a Key Stage 1 class where I took small groups for almost anything and had a brief to sort out anyone who needed extra help – and of course a lot of that was literacy.

Later, the school started setting all classes for English and mathematics by ability and I took a group of ten SEN children on my own. I had had no training for this, so I made my own decisions about what was best. It was very satisfying. As well as a lot of pre-literacy work we did very basic work on sounds and how to hold a pencil – things like that.

The Speech and Language Service has designed a scheme called Talk Time and I went on a one-day course to learn how to use it. It has really helped me to get the children talking more constructively.

I want, eventually, to be a teacher. I have just finished a foundation degree in early years work, studying part time at a local college where I learned a lot about literacy development. It cost £500 per year which I mostly paid myself, although I did get one £500 grant from the school and they claimed it back from SureStart.

If I do one more year – part time again through Kingston University – it will bring my degree up to a full BA. Then I can start teaching through the graduate teacher programme and be fully qualified in a couple of years.

3

Learning to read

Various methods of teaching children to read have moved in and out of favour in the last 50 years or so. In order to understand where we are now you need to know a little of the history.

Old phonics

Before about 1955 most children were taught to read using a system of sounding out letters. They learnt the sounds of each letter as well as their alphabetic names. Then, once they knew the sound that each letter often/sometimes/always makes, they could sound out words such as 'c-a-t' or 's-k-i-p'. It is easy to think of this as a golden age of literacy, but there were still many children – confined to very basic and banal books – who failed to become fluent readers.

'Look and say'

This became popular in the 1960s and involved training children to read whole words because many words cannot be sounded out. Words like 'comb', 'John', 'through', 'done' and 'rhinoceros' are not phonetic (written as they sound), for example. Experts say that 13 per cent of English words are not phonetic. So, many experts promoted whole-word recognition as the best method of teaching reading.

That means that you study the shape of a word like 'elephant' or 'playground,' memorize its pattern and remember it for next time. In fact, fast adult readers do use this method, of course. That is why it is easy to mistake 'polite notice' for 'police notice'. Once you can read fluently you no longer look at every letter.

Reading schemes like 'Janet and John' and the Ladybird scheme featuring Peter and Jane relied mostly on the 'look and say' method. Reinforcement work was done with cards with single words written on them. Known as 'flash cards', they were shown to the child who then had to recognize the shape and say what the word was.

Critics said that this was tantamount to asking the child to guess, rather than teaching him or her to break down the words systematically. (Many experts call this latter process 'decoding'– writing is like a code which the child has to crack.)

During the years that 'look and say' was widespread, phonics fell out of fashion, and gradually children's reading levels began to decline. Although most children eventually learned to read adequately, the 'look and say' method seemed to take them much longer. If you are between 20 and 50 this is probably more or less how you learned to read yourself.

Initial teaching alphabet

This was a short-lived and rather unfortunate experiment in the 1960s and 70s. Invented in 1961 by Sir James Pitman, whose grandfather Isaac Pitman devised shorthand, the initial teaching alphabet (ITA) was a complete system of writing and spelling using the 26 letters of the alphabet plus 14 more. It looked, at a glance, like a foreign language.

Children were supposed to master ITA and then seamlessly switch to conventional reading and spelling at the age of seven. Some did, but many failed to adjust. They found they could not read conventional text because it wasn't what they were used to. There are still adults who attended the schools which used ITA and who blame it for their ongoing difficulties with spelling and writing. It is possible that you are one of them.

The method effectively meant that children had to learn to

read and write twice. ITA was later recognized as unhelpful by most people and dropped. If you learn a spelling or word shape at the impressionable age of six it's quite difficult to unlearn it later, as you may know if you were an ITA victim.

'Real' books

In the 1980s and 90s there was a movement against reading schemes – books which systematically lead a child through various levels of vocabulary and language structures as he or she learns to read. Critics said that they were so dull that no child would be motivated to read them. The answer, they said, was to provide a large number of good, interesting books, known as 'real' books. The idea was that the children would then be motivated to read them and would, more or less, teach themselves to read. Some, of course did, but without a structured system many children progressed in reading only very slowly.

Mixed methods

When the National Curriculum arrived in 1988 it decreed that a range of methods should be used in teaching children to read. It recommended that phonics be part of this range, but no method was compulsory. Experts were beginning to say that a systematic approach to phonics was the only certain way of ensuring that every child learns to read as quickly and well as possible. They said that children were still left to flounder and that there was too much emphasis on guesswork rather than a systematic approach.

The literacy hour was introduced for primary schools in 1997, but it didn't insist on phonics either. Later the literacy hour became part of the Primary National Strategy, in parallel with the, then, new Key Stage 3 Strategy, but neither strategy insisted on phonics. It was stressed that phonics were desirable, but the choice of method was left to the schools.

More and more schools began to use one of the several published phonics schemes for the teaching of reading, but Ofsted inspectors often found that teachers (who went to school themselves in the 1960s, 70s, 80s or 90s) were not themselves sufficiently schooled in phonics to teach it well. In 1998 Ofsted reported that phonics was still being ignored in half of all schools.

The full circle

The wheel finally clicked back to its starting point in September 2006 when the rules were changed. It then became compulsory for all schools to use phonics to teach reading.

 Talk to adults you know (of different ages) about how they learned to read and their feelings about it. How can you use what your research has taught you to help the children you work with?

Twenty-first-century phonics

As a teaching assistant you need to know what phonics is about now that it is compulsory. Whether you are working with the youngest children in a primary school, or supporting SEN students at secondary level, some of your work will relate to the teaching and development of reading.

Phonics – the basics

Different schemes use slightly different versions of phonics (some are listed in Chapter 8). Analytic phonics isn't quite the same as synthetic phonics, for example, although there are broad similarities.

Analytic phonics concentrates on large chunks within words, especially when they rhyme, such as night, right, plight, fright or long, strong, gong, wrong. Synthetic phonics is a more structured approach which teaches children the sounds that letters or groups of letters make. The children then use these 'building blocks' to read and build words.

The important point to grasp is that words consist of:

1 Written graphemes which include:

- letters such as 'b' 'f' or 'r'
- vowel clusters in which letters ('a e i o u') are blended or synthesized together to create other sounds such as 'oa' and 'ee' (as in coat and peel)
- consonant clusters in which letters (the 21 in the alphabet which are not vowels) work together to create new sounds such 'th' in 'moth' and 'sl' in slip

2 Phonemes – these are single sounds formed by any of the above, so that when you sound out a word like strength it has four phonemes: str-e-ng-th. Rat has three: r-a-t. Animal has six because each letter is a separate phoneme: a-n-i-m-a-l. Sleep has three: sl-ee-p. There are about 42 different phonemes and 140 different letter combinations in English.

You may find the vocabulary varies slightly according to which scheme your school is using, but all are based on systematically introducing the children to graphemes and phonemes and teaching them the relationship between them.

 Think about words which can be read phonetically and those that can't. Make lists if it helps you to get the difference clear in your mind.

Reception and Key Stage 1: phonics activities

Whole-class teaching will usually involve learning new graphemes and phonemes, one by one, in a structured way until, after a few weeks or months, all the main ones have been covered. The teacher will probably do most of this him/herself.

Sometimes, as a team member, you may be asked to cover, or even to work with, the whole class as part of the planned programme of study for the class, possibly while the teacher does planning, preparation and assessment (PPA) work away from the classroom.

You will learn a lot about how best to handle whole-class teaching by watching the teacher, who may also ask you to assist by preparing literacy materials for the class to use. These could be, for example, work cards, mounted pictures or photocopied sheets. You may also be asked to order literacy materials from catalogues which the teacher (probably in consultation with colleagues) has selected for class use.

You will probably, however, spend most of your time working with smaller sections of the class in groups. If you are working with a group you could:

1 Work on hearing graphemes. Think of words beginning with a 'd' sound, such as door, dog, dig, and so on. Then, when they are ready, try getting the children to hear the 'd' sound at the end of words like lid, mud and nod.

2 Play the time-honoured 'I spy with my little eye something beginning with . . .' and take turns to guess (use the sound name 'f' rather than the letter name 'eff').

3 Help the children to practise putting together the graphemes they have learned. For example, if they know all the single alphabet letters and clusters 'br', 'oo' and 'ea' they can make cool, mean, beat, broom, mood, soon, Brad, and so on. Get them to write the words they can make too – if you end up with some invented words, so much the better. Write down some yourself and get the children to read them to you, or use letter tiles or brick, or letter magnets on a metal board.

Note: When you are writing or typing for beginner readers *never* use block capitals. Use a capital letter at the beginning of a word which needs it, like London or Charlie, because you don't want children to get used to seeing such words without their correct capitals. Otherwise use lower case letters. Block capitals do just that – they create a block of text and the word loses its visual shape. It is much easier to read Abigail or Saturday than ABIGAIL or SATURDAY.

4 Work on rhyme. If children have learned to read the word bit, then they can be helped to read sit, fit, hit, and so on. Get them to tell you. It doesn't matter if some of the words are invented like dit and vit. They are learning a lot about how words are built up. Use cut-up strips of paper, or something less flimsy such as tiles or bricks, to move the letters around. Or you might be able to use a computer or electronic white-board.

5 Be more ambitious with rhyming words as the children gain more knowledge and the grasp of phonemes builds up. Once they know the 'ch' cluster, for example, you can introduce church, much, touch, each and so on.

6 Play with clusters at the beginnings of words such as 'str' in string, strip, strap, strict. Once they know the 'sch' cluster, for instance, you can have school and, for the developing word-lovers, nice ones like scheme.

7 Get the children to write words they know on small pieces of paper and cut them out. Then they can lay or paste them onto a piece of paper to make a sentence or message. It can be very simple and phonetic, such as 'Jan and Kim ran in'. As the children get a better grasp of more words and patterns, obviously, it can get more complex.

8 Almost all children in all schools will have a reading book issued to them at the right level at this stage of their development. Hear them read aloud from it – many will also be doing

this at home with parents, but some won't. It can help to point to the words as the child reads, but don't do this if the child seems not to need it.

9 Play alphabet games. For example, get the children to take turns to think of something which begins with each letter of the alphabet. A more advanced version of this requires each player to think of something which begins with the letter the previous word ended with, so you get a sequence such as mat-tab-bun-nag-gap and so on. Or, once the child can visualize some basic spellings of words in which some letters aren't sounded, you can have sequences such as pipe-Edward-dumb-bone.

10 Teach them some tongue twisters, such as 'Peter Piper picked a peck of pickled peppers. If Peter Piper picked a peck of pickled peppers, where's the peck of pickled peppers Peter Piper picked?' Or 'She sells seashells on the seashore.' You can also make these up with the children, stressing that the words have to start with the same grapheme.

If you are assigned to Key Stage 1, think about how you might incorporate these ideas into your work.

Key Stage 2: phonics activities

Some children will now be beginning to struggle and you may find yourself working particularly with those. In a group of children who find it difficult to learn to read you could show them plenty of books and read to them as much as possible so that they enjoy things in books and get the message that reading is worthwhile. They may have missed out on this in the past.

Play word and letter games, such as going through the alphabet and trying to think of an item like a girl's name or something to eat beginning with each letter. So you get Anna, Bonita, Claire, Davina . . . or apple, beef burger, carrot, dhal . . .

Rework some of the word-building activities listed above for Key Stage 1, but don't let it get too 'babyish'. At Key Stage 2 the child would probably appreciate being allowed to do the word building in a more grown-up way, on a computer, for example.

If the children are making normal progress, or if you are asked to do some 'extension' work with a gifted and talented group, you could make a list of categories such as boy's name, girl's name, fruit or vegetable, something you wear and so on. (If the children are, say, in Year 6 or very able you can add challenging categories such as capital city or mammal.) Then choose a letter – if the letter is R, everyone has to think of each item beginning with that letter and, if they're able to, write it down. If not, you can find ways of doing this orally. So the first child might have Richard, Ruth, raspberry, ring (Riga, rabbit) while the second has Rajeev, Rachel, radish, raincoat (Rome, rat). The object is to get something no one else has thought of, so you need a points system – one point if someone else has the same, two points if it is the only one.

All the same word-building activities which work for Key Stage 1 will work at Key Stage 2, but let the shapes become increasingly more sophisticated. Explore words which rhyme, but which don't follow the same spelling patterns. Help the children to write a mini poem using words like beat, meet, receipt, deceit, Pete, making sure that everything is correctly spelled. Or have some fun with alliteration (starting several words with the same letter or grapheme) so that you use, for example, sprint, spring, sprinkle and sprout in the same sentence.

Make sure you hear the children reading aloud as often as possible.

The adjective game usually goes down well. In a small group the first person (you) says, for example, 'Gladys's cat is an adventurous cat.' The second says, 'Gladys's cat is an awful cat and the third, 'Gladys's cat is an amazing cat', and so on until everyone has had a turn. Then start the next round: 'Gladys's cat is a beautiful cat.' 'Gladys's cat is a bad cat' and so on until everyone has had a turn with every letter. It builds up vocabulary as well as concentrating the mind on which word starts with which letter. Make sure everyone says the whole sentence each time, because it has a fluent rhythm (and it's funny).

And listen for, work on and play with graphemes in the middle of words such as ex<u>pr</u>ess, un<u>pr</u>epared, sur<u>pr</u>ise or affe<u>ct</u>ed, disconne<u>ct</u>ed, ta<u>ct</u>less.

As their reading improves there's also a lot you can do with prefixes (syllables which go in front of another word to change its meaning) and suffixes (which go at the end of a word): <u>trans</u>late, <u>trans</u>port, <u>trans</u>plant or <u>inter</u>net, <u>inter</u>view, <u>inter</u>com (prefixes) and duck<u>ling</u>, sap<u>ling</u>, year<u>ling</u> or child<u>hood</u>, neighbour<u>hood</u>, parent<u>hood</u> (suffixes). It helps both reading and spelling to understand that words have different parts with different meanings.

Make up crosswords and word searches, or help the children to do ones you take from books or the Internet. They are a good way of consolidating reading and spelling skills.

 Can you use any of these ideas with your Key Stage 2 groups? Don't be afraid to adapt them.

Key Stage 3: phonics activities

If you are working with a small group on phonics at this stage then the pupils are by now, for whatever reason, almost certainly seriously behind. You will need tact and understanding to help them. They will appreciate the grown-up status of doing some of the work on computer if you can organize it. Try very hard not to be patronizing.

Work on listening skills. They won't be able to hear phonics in words until they have learnt to distinguish sounds. So get them to make sounds for surprise (Oooooo!), appreciation, (mmmmm) not fair, (Aaaah) and so on. You can make a game out of clapping the rhythm in words to 'hippopotamus' or 'Jessica'. And do anything else you can think of with music and sounds, appropriate to the age group, to develop careful listening.

Organize rhyming and sorting games, such as starting a statement and asking the pupil to complete it, 'Who gave the pearl to the —— (girl)?' Get them to sort pictures into piles according to the letter the items begin with. Choose pictures that are likely to appeal to the age group – footballers and lip gloss rather than teddy bears and trains.

Make a strip – perhaps on the computer – so that the pupils can make different words by moving it up and down over a central vowel. For example:

a
e
b i **d**
o
u

You can also make a game by creating words from an assortment of letters, perhaps on tiles. If you have an old, unwanted set of Scrabble or Boggle, the tiles work well for this.

As ever it's important to tell the children stories and share books with them. Help them to see that books are worth learning how to read. You can adapt any of the games and activities suggested above for Key Stages 1 and 2, but be sensitive to adolescence. As they progress, help them to read books which are at an appropriate reading level, but with age-related subject matter. Ransom Books do a range called Rainbow Readers which make a speciality of getting this balance right.

 Think about your own groups at school. Which of these ideas could help? Make a list of the things you want to try out.

Print size

Research has shown that children can often read a book more easily if the print is large. Sometimes a child will tell you that they found a book too difficult, but then read an 'easy version' and enjoyed it. The 'easy version' is the same. The only difference is the print size, but don't tell a child that until he or she has finished it. That is why there will probably be plenty of large-print books around in the classroom and in the school library.

When you are working with a group of children of any age learning to read, keep an eye on the print size of the material you are using. Many fiction and other books for children are available in large-print versions. If you are preparing material for learner readers, keep the print size large – it's very easy to do on a computer by adjusting the font.

Special educational needs

We've said quite a bit in this chapter about SEN because, obviously, if a child is still struggling to learn to read several years after most of his contemporaries have learned, there must be some kind of problem, difficulty or special need. And much of your work as a TA is likely to be with such children.

Whole books have, of course, been written about SEN children and all the many physical, environmental, social and behavioural reasons for their situation. But there are a few things which, in this context of literacy, you need to be aware of.

Since the Disability Discrimination Act became law in 2002 mainstream schools have become more inclusive. Many now have pupils with, for example, severe visual or aural disabilities or who need to use a wheelchair. As they learn to read, most of these children will need 'specialist' support, and that may be you. If so, you will need training from people who have expertise in working with the disability in question so that all children have equal opportunities to become literate. This can be very satisfying work.

Most children in mainstream schools with SEN have learning or behavioural difficulties (or both) rather than a physical disability. These include children with dyslexia and other similar conditions, children on the autistic spectrum or those whose background has traumatized them to such an extent that they are prevented from behaving conventionally which then holds back their learning. As you help them with literacy try to think of the latter group as troubled rather than troublesome and as having special needs rather than being 'badly behaved'. Remember that almost every child *can* learn to read if we can only find the right way of helping them.

In order to help children with dyslexia-type problems (and these range from very mild to extremely disabling) you need to make sure that instructions are very clear and that all the work is structured and planned step-by-step, as most phonics work now is. Many dyslexics have difficulty with self-organization so they will need patient help with things like getting themselves and their pens and pencils to the literacy session with you. A lot of research has been done on schemes such as those involving the use of coloured Perspex sheets to read through (this helps some dyslexics to read more easily). You will need to liaise with the teachers and any specialists working with the individual so that you know exactly how you can help.

'The autistic spectrum' is the term used to cover anyone with mild Asperger's syndrome at one end of the spectrum to severe autism at the other. Many children towards the milder end of the spectrum are being educated in mainstream schools. Some will almost certainly be in your small groups and it's all too easy to mistake their disability for naughtiness or 'bad behaviour'. You will probably be given a programme of work if you're helping them with their reading in a small group. Or, if you are supporting such children within the main class, then you will be told what you should do to help with their literacy – if not, ask. And if you want to understand how it feels to be autistic, read Mark Haddon's wonderful novel *The Curious Incident of the Dog in the Night-time*.

Gifted and talented children are now an identified group in schools and every school has to have a designated gifted and talented coordinator. Typically, such children learn to read early, finish work faster and ask very pertinent questions. But if they are not stretched and supported they can get bored and begin to underachieve. Sometimes they develop behaviour problems and have in the past been mistaken for children with learning difficulties. In a sense they, too, have SEN. As TA you need to be aware of who they are, make sure that they are never left with nothing to do and have plenty of 'extension' activities ready. That means, for example, interesting books that they can discuss with you when they've read them or opportunities to research further on the Internet what they've read. Or sometimes it's appropriate to encourage them to help other children.

Doing the job

Carol Dowling is a teaching assistant at Collingwood School, South Woodham Ferrers, Essex. She started this job in 2000 having been a midday meals supervisor for 19 years.

I have worked with various age groups, but now I work with 9–11-year-olds in Years 5 and 6. Sometimes I take individuals, but mostly I work with a group of about six children with SEN. An individual education plan (IEP) has been worked out for each of them because they are falling behind with their literacy.

The school uses a reading scheme published by Heinemann called Storyworlds. All the key words are there and the phonics work is inbuilt. These are very good books and you can really see the children make progress with their reading in these small groups.

We also use books published by Rising Stars. They do a series for boys called *Boys Rule* and another for girls called *Girls Rock*. These are written specifically for children who are in Years 3–6 but whose reading is still at level 2 or below. The children like these and they work very well.

I've been interested in this sort of work for some time because I like to keep my brain alive and want to keep active. I did a course for specialist teachers' assistants at Chelmsford College in 1998 before I started. It took one year during which I spent two or three half-days in schools and one full day at college each week. It gave me a lot of useful information and experience.

4

Writing

Writing starts as soon as a child can hold a crayon, and awareness of it probably begins even earlier. A baby who sees a parent or carer reading a notice or a book is, at some level, learning that the adult is absorbing meaning from paper. And as soon as the child begins to make marks on paper he or she is on the way to becoming a writer.

Early drawing

A child with a crayon is starting to develop the hand control that will eventually be needed to form small letters. He or she is also beginning to practise shapes – all 26 letters of the alphabet are based on circles or part circles, strokes and dots. This is just what the beginner draws on the paper.

So you, the teaching assistant, should encourage drawing and art work in the youngest children. It's valuable in itself, but it's also an essential stepping stone on the journey to writing. Meanwhile, you can help the youngest children by playing games which help to strengthen the muscles in the fingers and hands, for example, sorting beads, singing songs with actions, storytelling using finger puppets.

Shaping letters

As the drawing develops, those circles and strokes can gradually be formed into big letters – usually the first is the initial letter of the child's name such as S for Susannah, I for Ishmael.

To begin with the children will not be able to write their letters small. They can colour their big letters in, so you could end up with illuminated letters for the classroom wall.

Try to avoid the disjointed 'ball and stick' approach to forming letters. In the past children were often taught that a 'b', for example, is a circle with a straight line next to it or that a 'g' is a circle with a hook underneath. Instead of this, encourage the children to shape letters from one continuous, flowing line. Keep the crayon on the paper – which may mean going over some bits of the letter twice. This is important because of a new development in the teaching of handwriting which we shall come to shortly.

Progressing to a pen or pencil

If children are very young or very immature they will not be ready to hold a narrow pencil or pen. If you force them before they're ready they will soon find that writing hurts because it causes cramp and other problems. That, naturally, will put them off writing, which is the last thing we want. So, at the early stages you need to go gently and, probably, at the child's own pace.

As the drawing evolves into writing and finger skills improve, encourage the child to hold the pencil or crayon with the barrel lying loosely in the angle between the thumb and first finger. The first finger should rest bent on the top of the pencil, which is held from the sides by the tip of the thumb and the side of the second finger. Handwriting experts call this the 'tripod position'. There are special pens and pencils on the market and in use in some schools which can help. These writing implements have a triangular shaped barrel with shallow concave grooves so that the children's small digits sit naturally where they should.

Learning the tripod position – and establishing good habits – will solve many problems later. A child who holds a pencil too tightly, or who chooses some other form of grip, will probably have difficulty writing at length. He or she may end up as an adult with repetitive strain injury too. If this is not how you hold your own pen or pencil, this might be a good moment to train yourself out of bad habits. Setting a good example is a teacher's and TA's strongest weapon.

Teaching methods

Now to that new development in the teaching of handwriting. Until about the 1920s all children were taught joined-up – or 'cursive' (literally 'running') writing – from the very first words they wrote. Then educationists decided that it would be easier for children if they were first taught to write using separated letters, like the ones they see in printed books. Then, once that was mastered, the child would be allowed, or encouraged, to join up his letters in writing. And for 80 years or so that was how nearly everyone learned.

The problems with this method are that:

- you have to learn to write twice
- the single letters most people were taught had no links or hooks (like the sans serif or Ariel fonts on a modern computer) so that it was very difficult for children to adapt to joining up because they had to learn a new way of forming the letters
- spaced letters make it hard to distinguish between upper case and lower case letters when the shape is the same, as with 's' or 'v', for example
- many children were not taught how to join up, but left to their own devices. Some, therefore, went on writing – and still do – in a laborious, separate-letter style which is very slow and may, some research has suggested, make it harder to spell correctly
- even people who mastered some form of joined-up writing often had very untidy, unattractive, even illegible (because letters are badly formed) handwriting in adult life.

So there is now a move back to teaching children cursive handwriting much earlier. The result seems to be a higher standard of handwriting among nearly all the children in the schools which have adopted this policy, so more and more schools are switching to it.

When you are helping children to begin to form letters, encourage them to make them flowing, one-line creations. You can map a path with dots and help a child to trace it, for example. Every letter needs a hook or serif so that it can be attached to another letter. The hook is part of the flow of the letter. It isn't something added on as an afterthought.

This may not come naturally to you as you were almost certainly taught 'ball and stick' yourself, so you will have to practise! There are a number of good books, worksheets and websites which will help you. Try *Handwriting: the way to teach it* by Rosemary Sassoon (Paul Chapman Publications, 2003 edition). Find others – there are too many to list – by putting 'cursive writing' into a search engine or browsing in a large bookshop. Many of them are American in origin but equally applicable to the UK.

Pupils with specific handwriting problems

Some schemes are designed especially for older children in Key Stage 2 or 3 who have already developed handwriting problems with which they need help. It is important to make handwriting activities fun and satisfying for this older age group so that they can see real improvement in their efforts.

They may already be feeling pretty demoralized. Don't make it any worse. One tactic, if your own handwriting is less than perfect, is to take the line that 'we're all going to work together to improve our handwriting because mine isn't very good either'. Or show them some before and after handwriting samples from a group you have worked with in the past.

Some of the available worksheets and schemes could also help if you are working with children learning English as a second, or additional, language. If they have begun their education using a language such as Chinese or Arabic, children will have to learn to form completely different sorts of letters.

There is a lot of useful advice and information about handwriting on the National Handwriting Association's website: www.nha-handwriting.org.uk/

Left-handedness

About one child in eight is left-handed or, to be more accurate, left-dominant. She or he will probably walk with the left foot first and be stronger in the left eye than the right too. There is absolutely nothing wrong with this, of course, and long gone are the bad old days when adults cruelly forced left-handed children to write with the other hand and regarded left-handedness as sinister. (The word sinister actually comes from *sinistra*, the Latin word for left, which illustrates the old attitude well.)

But you, as TA, would do well to keep a particular eye on left-handed children as they learn the mechanics of writing. Encourage them to keep the paper in front of them rather than placing it a long way to one side. It should be angled about 30 degrees to the left. Help the child to hold the pencil in the same way as right-handed friends do. Left-handers are inclined to devise their own clumsy methods because they cannot make the conventional ones work for them and they don't always get the help they need. I have seen left-handed adults, for example, writing by curving the left arm round the top of a piece of paper and angling the hand from the top towards the bottom of the paper – almost writing backwards – so that they can see what they're writing.

You are well placed to try to stop such habits developing in the very young. You should also make sure that they have plenty of working space. If a right-hander sits too close to a left-hander the two will jog each other because their working arms are side by side. That is not, of course, an argument for segregating the left-handers, merely for making sure that they are not squashed.

Adults as scribes

Very young children often know what they want to write but cannot yet write it, so they need an adult to write it down for them. In education jargon this process is called 'scribing' and the adult who does the writing is a 'scribe'. For example, children might want their daily news recorded, or a caption put under a picture for display. As TA it will quite often be your job to 'scribe' for the children.

Listen carefully to what they say and write it in a way that can be read by the more advanced readers in the class or by visitors from other classes. A single sentence is usually enough. If the child can manage it he or she might sign what you have written by writing his or her name at the bottom. The work is all part of showing the children that writing is important and valued by grown-ups.

Forming words

Once children can form letters and are beginning to read words by using phonics there is almost unlimited scope for writing.

The child's own name should always be the first target – the given name first. (It's best, incidentally, to avoid the term 'Christian name' in school because children from non-Christian cultures don't have them. 'First name' is tricky too, because Chinese people, for example, put the chosen name after the family name. 'Given name' seems to fit the bill.) Work on the family name as soon as the child is comfortable with writing the given name. Soon they should be able to write Susan Elkin or Panjit Singh without too much help.

They will also want to write words like Mum, Dad, Nan and the names of siblings. Make sure that you know how siblings' and other relations' names are spelled. Many can be spelled more than one way (Catherine, Katherine, Kathryn, Catharine or Leigh, Lee, Lea, for example) and names from a culture other than your own are a potential minefield. If you're in any doubt, ask the child's parent or whoever brings them to school.

Write words with gaps in, such as d-g, h-n, shar-, -us, put pictures beside the words and ask the children to fill in the spaces with letters. You can very easily devise worksheets along these lines using clipart or, if you prefer, draw your own or cut little pictures out of magazines and photocopy the result. You can then use the same ones as often as you like. Just run off more.

Ask children to write, for example, park, nest, match and pink spaced across the top of a sheet or do it for them. Underneath they should list as many words as they can by changing the first letters – so you get: dark, bark, mark; best, pest, rest; latch, hatch, thatch; drink, link, think and so on. Then they can decorate the edges of the paper.

Give them word openings such as 'thr', 'gr', 'qu', 'bl'. Ask them to list as many words as they can using this beginning, so you get: throw, three, throne; growl, grab, grey; quick, queen, quiz; blue, blood, black. Or do it with word endings such as 'ing', 'end', 'ake' so that you get: sing, ring, king; bend, friend, lend; cake, make, quake. Again, let them decorate the rest of the paper.

Almost any game or activity you can devise which encourages children to put letters together to form words and write them down is likely to be useful and to support other work the children are doing. Let your imagination rip!

Think about how you might use the writing games and activities suggested here with the pupils you work with. Can you add any more?

Sentence building

Words are the building blocks of sentences. As soon as a child can make words he or she can begin to put them in order.

In practice children can start to write sentences as soon as they can write a word or two. Use the child's own name and start with the simplest phonetic words, so you get sentences like, 'Jamila runs' or 'Craig sits'.

Get the children to write and illustrate their sentences. Then you can move on to slightly more complex sentences such as, 'Mum and I went to the shops' or 'Owen has eaten his apple'. You may want to write some of these for the children to copy or they can make them up. From there it's only a short hop to writing for real.

Writing for 'real' purposes

Instead of merely practising with letters, words and contrived sentences you can encourage children at all Key Stages to write:

- news
- stories
- letters
- postcards
- emails
- diaries
- greetings cards
- articles for the school magazine or website
- notices for the classroom
- poems
- instructions
- plays
- shopping lists
- recipes
- notes

- factual accounts
- records of findings or observations
- many other forms of writing.

In practice pupils will probably have been set some of these to write by the teacher. Your job as TA will be to help them to produce what they have been told to do. This could mean:

- helping with the spellings of problem words
- assisting with thinking of the right word for something
- helping with punctuation, especially upper case letters for beginnings of sentences, and full stop, question mark or exclamation mark for sentence endings
- helping with grammar, especially nouns and verbs
- offering the occasional idea for a story which gets 'stuck'
- suggesting a rhyme for a poem
- advising children on where they can get information
- helping with ICT if a computer is being used
- reading through written work which is finished or under way and providing feedback.

Note: If your own education was a long time ago and/or you feel, for any reason, less than confident about offering spelling, punctuation, grammar and vocabulary advice to children, you might find the *Compact Oxford English Dictionary for Students* (Oxford University Press, 2006 edition) a useful reference book to keep handy. The main part of the dictionary is very clearly set out with straightforward word meanings, many of which are illustrated in sentences. In the centre of the dictionary is an excellent section with blue-edged pages called 'Brush up your English'. It sets out the basics of grammar and punctuation in a very clear and accessible way.

Children, especially in small literacy groups, may also be engaged in writing something which you as TA have set or suggested directly. Or the children, especially if they are part of a gifted and talented group, may have decided for themselves that they are going to write about a particular topic in a particular way, perhaps as part of a project.

At Key Stage 3 your literacy group may be using its time with you to work on writing about something – probably on a worksheet – which has arisen in a subject-specific lesson such as science or history.

 Think about all the different sorts of writing which the children you work with are expected to do. Can you add to the list given above (on page 48)?

Frameworks for writing

In literacy teaching a framework means a diagram with boxes which are empty or contain just a few outline words. Each box represents a paragraph and the child has to fill in the boxes. Many teachers now encourage children to write by using a framework to hang a story or other writing on. For many pupils, using a framework is a lot less daunting than sitting down with a blank sheet of paper or screen. In effect it means that the basic shape of the story is laid out, but the pupil fills in the details.

It can be a useful way of helping a child to shape a piece of writing. The outline supports his or her ideas. Sometimes teachers devise their own frameworks in which case you, of course, will have access to them in order to help the children.

There are many published schemes offering frameworks for writing, often with photocopiable worksheets for the children to use (such as *Writing Frameworks: Easy-to-use structures for creating confident, successful writers* by David Whitehead, published by Pembroke Publishing, 2003). If your school is using such a scheme you will need to familiarize yourself with it. The use of frameworks for writing is encouraged by National Curriculum as well as by the Primary and Secondary National Strategies.

 Try devising a writing framework to help you to understand how they work. You could then try it out on a child.

Creative writing and creative reading

When a child (or adult) reads, he or she has to use imagination. The writer writes and the reader reads. Both are creating images in their heads – but not necessarily the same ones.

In school we try to develop children as imaginative readers to the highest possible level. We also aim to develop the creativity of their writing. The two are closely connected because *reading*:

- provides ideas for the reader's own writing
- teaches new words
- shows many ways in which words can be moved about to create interesting sentences
- can provide the facts needed for a piece of writing (for example, the date of an invention or the colours of the rainbow which can be found in a reference book or read on the Internet).

A child's *writing* meanwhile:

- provides something for another creative reader to read
- shows clearly what the child has read or likes to read
- can be a way of communicating the pleasure of reading to someone else – in a book review, for example.

So, you as TA need to be aware of the importance of reading and books when you are encouraging children to write and/or helping them with their writing. Consider, for example, getting children at any age across Key Stages 1–3 to:

- write a poem modelled on one they've read
- write a short account of facts they have learned from a book they have read – for example, what happened to the people who supported the king in mid-seventeenth-century England after reading Sally Gardner's *I, Coriander*? Almost any fiction book has some factual background
- note down six new words learned from, say, a Harry Potter book
- email a friend to tell him or her about a book they have enjoyed
- write a letter or postcard perhaps to a grandparent, commenting on a book
- keep a list of books read – a reading log with titles accurately written. Include publisher, author and other details. This is a good habit for young readers to get into. It means they can easily find books they've read in the past when they want to look at them again. And it helps teach them to value reading
- write sequels and other additions to books they've read, such as another chapter or a new story about one of the characters
- make notes based on non-fiction books
- write to the author (c/o the publisher) of any book they have enjoyed, congratulating/thanking him or her and asking polite questions. Many authors will answer children's letters, which is very exciting for the letter writer.

Using a keyboard as a writing tool

Writing is no longer limited to what you can do with a pen or pencil. Computers and keyboards are now part of everyday life. Most professional writers use them. Children will use them at work and almost everywhere else in the future, so they should learn how to make the best use of them too – as well, of course, as learning to write by hand.

What the children write can then be read on a computer screen, projected onto an electronic whiteboard, emailed to someone else (you, for example, so you can read it elsewhere), posted on the school intranet, printed out, and so on. You can edit it on screen with the pupil – you don't need a red pen and the pupils can see their work improve rather than having it 'marked'.

There is, however, absolutely no point in writing, say, a story or poem on paper with a pen and then laboriously copying it onto the computer. The trick is to encourage the children to think at the keyboard and let their fingers become the pen. That means they type as the ideas flow – just as I'm writing this book. The words are appearing on my screen as they form in my mind. I have a few handwritten notes – headings and book titles and so on – in a notebook at my side, but otherwise I'm 'composing at the keyboard'.

With encouragement, children at Key Stages 1 and 2 will adapt to working in this way very quickly, especially if the school also teaches touch-typing so that the children are quick and accurate on the keyboard. By the time they get to Key Stage 3, writing with a keyboard should be second nature.

Some of the advantages of keyboard writing are that the young writer can:

- move words, sentences and paragraphs around
- consult the computer's dictionary or thesaurus (make sure the setting is UK not US)
- use the grammar check
- use the spellcheck (UK setting), although as you help them be aware that computer spellchecks are not foolproof because they sometimes 'correct' a word to one which isn't what the writer meant – sometimes with hilarious results. It's useful for checking typing errors, though
- link literacy with curriculum ICT work
- get facts needed to inform the writing easily by consulting the Internet at the same time

- often work more quickly – many pupils can type faster than they write with a pen
- save the work and readily return to it later
- produce very neat, professional-looking work which is satisfying and good for self-esteem.

Some children write better quality stories, poems and other forms of creative writing on computer than they ever would with pen and paper. For reasons it's hard to pin down technology seems to liberate creativity for some people.

Writing activities for small groups

If you are working with a group of children who need extra practice with their writing:

- Make a clear distinction between the mechanics of handwriting (or typing) and the process of original writing. We tend to use the same word for both, which is a bit confusing. There might be times when you want to do a handwriting or typing exercise with the group or with individuals because problems have emerged in class. But when you are trying to get them to write imaginatively, informatively or whatever, don't nag about the mechanics of how to form letters because it will distract them from the content of what they're writing. The aim, of course, is that eventually they will be able to do both at once.
- Give lists of words and challenge them to make up the most interesting or funny sentences they can from them. You can do this at any age, but if the children are older or particularly able make the words more challenging. So for a very young or limited group you might give them: Marie, bat, an, the, held, sat, asked, funny, quickly. For a more advanced group you could list: principal, wondered, reason, energy, mouldering, the, an, lay, personal, it's, and

so on. They don't need to use all the words in every sentence.

▨ Use an object as the starting point for a story – a large shell, an old map, a broken bottle, a football shirt or whatever. Show it to them and encourage discussion – 'Who might be using this map?' 'A pirate?' 'Where is he and where does he want to go?' Then let them write a story or a poem in any way they like. You can start this off as a group, working out how this story will go, and then they can write it as individuals.

▨ Show them an object such as a very old newspaper, a large knobbly potato or a hand-knitted cardigan. Let them touch it, smell it, hear it rustle, as well as see it. Their task is to describe it accurately in as few sentences as possible – as if for someone from Mars who has no experience of such an object.

▨ Set them to practise writing instructions for everyday tasks such as making a piece of toast and Marmite or sharpening a pencil. The idea is to make the instructions thorough and logical. You can work though the stages with them first.

▨ Get them to describe a real-life experience. It can be something very ordinary, such as the rain on the way to school this morning or today's school dinner queue (good for Key Stage 3). It need not be very long. The idea is to create a lively read. Anything can be made to seem fascinating if it's told in an entertaining way, as all journalists know.

SEN writing activities

With a Key Stage 1 SEN group
Include games and activities which involve moving the fingers in particular ways, such as using Lego or using the fingers for actions in rhymes. Almost all children who need extra help with writing also need help to improve 'motor skills' or controlled body movement.

More specifically, do plenty of handwriting work following up on what the teacher has done with the whole class. If the child is ready, help him/her to write his/her name and simple words. But don't force it. Try using pictures and get the child to write down some of what he/she hears and sees – possibly just a list of items. Or 'scribe' what the child would like to write and show him/her word by word what you have written. Use any worksheets that are being used in the class to encourage the child to put words together into sentences. You may need to help with this very slowly, step by step.

Remember that a child suffering from attention deficiency or hyperactivity will need to be given many small tasks rather than one big one which could seem daunting.

With a Key Stage 2 SEN group

Be aware that dyslexia may now be emerging in some children. It can be diagnosed at Key Stage 1, but typically it isn't fully recognized until a child is eight or nine at the earliest. That means that you, the TA, need to make every instruction simple and clear:

- Today we are going to practise writing sentences.
- Write your name here, please.
- Write a sentence beginning with the word James.
- Put a full stop at the end of your sentence.
- Remember that 'necessary' has one 'c' and two 's's – one collar and two sleeves.

You may even find yourself 'translating' for these children what the class teacher has said to the whole class in a less direct style.

Many dyslexic children find it difficult to organize themselves and their possessions. You can help them with this by reminding them what they need, but try to make them realize that they have to take responsibility too. They won't always have a friendly TA to do their remembering for them, so think of ways of helping them to remember. One technique is to count the number of items a child should have, such as pen, pencil, notebook, reading book and glasses – five items. Then you can say, 'How many things should you have with you, Ella? Have you counted?'

Read to children as much as you can. The more language they hear, the more likely they are to catch up – and that applies, in particular, to pupils learning English as a second language. If you have got even two minutes left at the end of session after packing up, read aloud a poem, joke, paragraph from a newspaper, opening of an exciting book or a short piece from a reference book which has caught your eye. Encourage them, if they can, to write about what they have heard read. Many are likely to be behind with their own reading so they will be short of writing ideas.

Have some handwriting practice worksheets to hand. Some will need help with this, as well as with what to write.

With a Key Stage 3 SEN group

There are two big differences at Key Stage 3. First, any child who still needs help with writing now may be demoralized, and behaviour problems are quite likely to go with that too. Second, because the secondary school curriculum is usually subject-based you may have to help with writing tasks relating to several different subjects.

Alternatively you may be attached to a department – such as science or English – and help children withdrawn from a lesson or working as a group within the class only in those subjects.

The aim, of course, is to give these children the same access to learning that the rest of the class has – and that includes helping them to write things down. You will probably:

- help with spelling
- suggest words
- help children to fill in charts and grids with written words
- show pupils where they can find what they need to write down (in a textbook, on the board, for example).

Nothing succeeds like success. Praise their efforts so that pupils realize that their achievements, even quite modest ones, are valued. Then they are more likely to be motivated to try harder to succeed again.

Doing the job

Julia Skinner is in her 50s and has three grown-up children. She is a teaching assistant at Crofton Secondary School in the London Borough of Lewisham.

I work under the head of English (not the special needs department) and there are two of us who take groups out of class for literacy work. I started here in 1995 without qualifications (although I had done some voluntary and some paid work at Perrymount Primary School). Since then I have done several City and Guilds courses for TAs – specializing in literacy.

We have about 70 youngsters in Years 7, 8 and 9 who need extra help. They are the ones who haven't achieved level 4 in reading as they are expected to at the age of 11. Many have English as a second language, and we have 53 different first languages in the school. All these children need encouragement and support with reading and writing.

Secondary school pupils are often reluctant to admit they have not been coping with literacy. And they often get made fun of by the others, which makes it even harder for them.

Most of the pupils I work with are capable. It's just that reading and writing didn't 'click' with them when they were younger. I work hard to build up their confidence and to help them to have fun with literacy activities which they enjoy. It pays off. They almost all move up a level between Year 7 and Year 8.

It's a very interesting – but challenging! – job.

5

Developing real readers

Nearly all children – without severe disability – eventually learn to turn the squiggles on the page, paper or noticeboard into words. They may, sadly, not be very quick or fluent, but when they see 'Toilets', 'Exit' or 'Cheese sandwich £1.50' they know what it means. Very few children in the modern, developed world reach adulthood in a state of total illiteracy.

At the ages of six, seven, eight or later they can stumble through a passage from a book while an adult listens. It can be hard to say how much sense they are making of their reading at this stage because they are concentrating on laborious decoding, but they are coming out with words which correspond to the ones on the paper. So they can read?

Well, yes and no. They can decode certainly. And National Curriculum tests at ages 7, 11 and 14 will, to an extent, show that they understand what they are reading. But I would argue that actually this is not reading and that 'real reading' is what you learn to do once you've cracked the code.

Think about driving. Passing the test is not the end of your driving career. It's the beginning. Once you've got that piece of paper in your hand you can drive to, for example, Yorkshire if you live in Kent (or to Kent, if you live in Yorkshire) on your own and really get the hang of the finer points of motoring. And it's just the same with reading. First we need to teach them to decode and then help them to become 'fast-lane' readers.

Sadly, this is a stage and a concept which too often gets neglected. It's easy to think that once a child can read you don't have to do any more because the job is done. You can tick the reading box and hurry on to the next thing. But if you passed your driving test, walked out of the test centre and didn't get into a car's driving seat again for five or ten years you would probably find that the skill had gone because you hadn't consolidated and developed it. In other words: use it or lose it.

TAs have a big part to play in transforming new readers into real readers so that they can, and do, read everything they need or want to for the rest of their lives.

Subvocalizing

When a child first learns to read he says each word aloud. It's the only way to prove to himself and to any adult who is helping – perhaps a TA 'hearing reading' – that the word has been read.

Then, once independent reading begins the child, mostly, stops reading words aloud – although you can often see a beginner's lips moving which is still, effectively, reading aloud. This is known as 'subvocalizing' and many children and adults never stop doing it – which makes them very slow readers. A subvocalizer reads every word aloud to himself inside the head but without speaking. Even if the lips aren't moving he is articulating every word without making audible sounds.

A subvocalizer is still in the shallow end of reading – maybe even hanging on to the bar at the side of the pool. A strong, 'deep-end' reader can read quickly for meaning, without having to 'translate' each individual word into a sound. The brain learns to convert signs seen by the eye into meaning without consciously passing through the medium of spoken or heard words.

The aim for any TA, teacher or parent working with children is to move them on from subvocalizing. If children get stuck at this stage they will never read effortlessly. As with swimming, practice is the most important thing. They need blocks of time every day when they read independently and silently. And as with any other skill, the more you do it the faster you get. It's partly a matter of acquiring the confidence to stop using subvocalizing as a prop – and letting go.

Another trick for building up confident, fluent reading is to encourage the children to read quite a lot of material which is slightly below their reading level so that they can read it easily. This cannot be their only reading, of course, but it should be a large part of it.

It is important to understand that we all read at different levels too. You might enjoy reading Charles Dickens (I do) but choose for a long flight with noise and distraction an easy read, by, say, Maeve Binchy. And I think – as with many people in my generation – it was Enid Blyton who taught me to stop sub-vocalizing because I wanted to race on through the excitement of the story. For many, J.K. Rowling and Harry Potter do the same job today.

As TA you can help too by giving a child, say, a paragraph or two to read, but limit the time that he or she has to read it. For fun you could read the same passage at the same time with the same time limit. Then take it away and talk about what has been read. Encourage the child to skim the whole page for meaning quickly. Do this only with material which is quite easy for the child concerned – short magazine articles work well for this, or something from a suitable newspaper such as Newsademic.com, a digital, international newspaper for 9–16s (see www.newsademic.com) with plenty of very accessible short articles.

And be aware that subvocalizing can also be useful. It is a skill we all go back to if a piece of reading is particularly chal-lenging – complicated instructions or something in a foreign language we have only basic knowledge of, for example. Many times, with impenetrable instructions (think flat-pack furni-ture!), I have found myself not just subvocalizing but actually reading aloud in an attempt to make sense of what I am trying to read. So subvocalizing is part of a literate person's reading armoury but is, in a sense, a disability if it's your *only* reading strategy.

That is why we need to move children on from it. However, it's quite a hard concept to explain to children, who won't probably understand or recognize that there is more than one way of reading until, suddenly, they find the brakes are off and they are whizzing through pages of print without subvocalizing.

Think about how you read yourself and talk to other adults about it. You will probably find several who still habitually subvocalize.

Reading what you want them to read

If you want to encourage children to read you need to show a real interest in what they are reading, That means that you will probably have to take home and read a large number of children's books. But don't worry, this is no hardship. Some of them are wonderful. And bearing in mind that publishers classify all readers under 16 as 'children', some of the children's books at the upper end, which Key Stage 3 pupils might be reading, (by Aidan Chambers or Linda Newbery for instance) are pretty adult.

From thousands of possibilities I've picked just a handful of premier league fiction titles and authors to suggest here. Start your journey into children's fiction with some of these if you haven't already read them. Some have been around some time and become modern children's classics, while others are quite recent. I've grouped them very approximately into Key Stage 2 and Key Stage 3 (because these are the levels at which some children need reading development rather than reading teaching), but be aware that these age ranges are very fluid. A nine-year-old will sometimes happily read a book more usually read by 13-year-olds and vice versa. Reading levels, ability and interest haven't got much to do with chronological age, and no two children are the same.

Key Stage 3 is particularly tricky because a boy or girl

starting in Year 7 might still read quite 'babyish' books. Three years – and an adolescence – later, at the end of Year 9, he or she may be reading books published for adults. Children all develop at different rates, so it is impossible to generalize across the whole Key Stage. Once you, as TA, have read some of the books you will develop a feeling for what is likely to appeal to which child and therefore what to recommend.

Key Stage 2

- *Skellig* by David Almond
- *The Silver Sword* by Ian Seraillier
- *Goodnight Mister Tom* by Michelle Magorian
- *Simone's Letters* by Helen Pielichaty
- *Tom's Midnight Garden* by Philippa Pearce
- *I, Coriander* by Sally Gardner
- *The Amazing Story of Adolphus Tips* by Michael Morpurgo
- *The Cat Mummy* by Jacqueline Wilson.

Key Stage 3

- *Tamar* by Mal Peet
- *Wolf* by Gillian Cross
- *The Foreshadowing* by Marcus Sedgwick
- *His Dark Materials* by Philip Pullman (three books)
- *The Hobbit* by J. R. R. Tolkien
- *Private Peaceful* by Michael Morpurgo
- *Noughts and Crosses* by Malorie Blackman.

Look too for books suitable for both Key Stages by:

- Anne Fine
- Robert Westall
- Robert Cormier
- Kevin Crossley-Holland
- Ursula Le Guin
- Adèle Geras

- Geraldine McCaughrean
- Bernard Ashley.

Setting an example

Children imitate adults. That is how they learn. And, sadly, they emulate the bad things as well as the good.

So, if they see adults absorbed in, and enjoying, books they get the message that reading is a grown-up thing to do. If, on the other hand adults in positions of influence (teachers, TAs, parents) say they are too busy to read because they have other more important things to do, then children are likely to stop reading at the earliest opportunity because it 'feels' like grown-up behaviour.

This is a very significant part of the reason why so many children read quite enthusiastically at Key Stage 2 but give it up as soon as they hit puberty. It is, therefore, vital for the development of literacy that children see lots of adult 'role models' reading books. Sadly they may not have this at home (although many will) so school has to compensate and you, as TA, can do a lot to help.

Always have a book with you that you are in the process of reading – sticking out of your bag or on the corner of your desk. Make it clear that you take your book wherever you go in case you get an odd moment. Let the children see you reading for pleasure.

If the class or group is reading silently, then you read too. If you undertake any other activity you are suggesting that it is more important than reading – it isn't (except in the most dire emergency, such as tending a sick child). Talk a lot about books and read informally with the children.

Why not become a book eccentric ('book buff', 'book nut')? Make fun of yourself. Present yourself as someone who never leaves home bookless, who has sold your TV set, who sometimes forgets to wash up because you're so deep in your book, who often can't remember whether you've read the book or seen the film . . . and so on. The children will laugh at, and with, you, but they will also admire your respect for the printed word and some will copy it.

Tell them about books you enjoyed when you were their age and/or about books your own children have enjoyed. Listen to what pupils tell you about books they have read and you haven't. Make a point of reading some of them and then feeding back your thoughts. It is very gratifying for a child if an adult heeds a recommendation and spends time exploring it. It gives reading real status.

The blunt truth is that if you are not seen to be a committed reader you will never be really successful in encouraging children to read widely and keenly. Lip service doesn't work. Neither does 'Do as I say but not as I do'. It's no good just telling children that reading is 'A Good Thing'. They need to see adults excitedly doing it.

 When did you last read a children's book? If you were to read one a week – and most of them are quite short – you would have read 52 after a year. And you would have a good personal 'bank' of books to discuss with the children you work with.

Boys

Most people working in education know that it is harder to persuade boys to read than girls. And there is a lot of research evidence to prove it. National Curriculum test results at Key Stages 2 and 3, for example, always show that for English girls are, on average, several percentage points better than boys.

There are a number of reasons:

■ Boys under about 16 are a few months behind girls of the same age in terms of physical and mental development. Some boys get left behind in literacy, even at Key Stage 1, as the girls forge ahead.

- All children should be physically active, of course, and opportunities must be equal, but there is a slight tendency for boys to be more physically active than girls. That means that in some cases the boys find it harder to sit still and concentrate.
- Fewer adult men read for pleasure than adult women – especially fiction – so some boys do not see male role models (fathers, grandfathers, uncles) reading at home. And in many homes there are, anyway, no men.
- Only about 20 per cent of Key Stage 2 teachers are male – and even fewer TAs – so boys don't see much male reading behaviour at school either.
- Some boys are turned off by fiction which they regard (perhaps influenced by the non-reading males in their lives) as soppy and girlish.
- There is a shortage of high-quality non-fiction on the market to offer boys instead.

As a TA, be aware that:

- some male authors are now deliberately writing fiction books with boy-appeal. Anthony Horowitz's Alex Rider books (now being made into films such as *Stormbreaker*) are a good example. So are most of Alan Gibbons's books
- boys do not, in general, want to read books in which the main characters are girls. They are put off by anything with a girl's name on the cover – especially if it's pink! (But these are published in large numbers because a publisher wanting to make profits knows that they will sell – to girls.)
- boys are often happy to read magazines instead of books
- non-fiction books may appeal. Encourage them to look for books about subjects that they are interested in. Football and computers (and dinosaurs and planets at Key Stage 2) are likely contenders, but don't stereotype. You may find the boys you're working with have plenty of other inter-

ests, so talk to them. Remember too that there is at least one specialist magazine published for almost every interest you can think of.

- there is interesting non-fictional information on all subjects on the Internet. Print it off for boys.

You – and the Key Stage 2 class teacher – need to find male role model readers. If neither of you is male, swap classes with a male colleague occasionally for reading activities. Invite male readers into school from outside to talk to the children. Think along the same lines at Key Stage 3. The school will be larger, and there are more men working in secondary schools, so there are almost certainly male colleagues to call on – both TAs and teachers.

Think about the men and boys you know, both at work and elsewhere. What is their attitude to reading? Do they view it differently from the women and girls you know?

School libraries and bookshops

Almost all schools have some sort of library. In a primary school it will probably be managed by one of the teachers, perhaps assisted by one or more TAs. At secondary level it is more likely – but not inevitable – that there is a full-time, professionally qualified librarian running the library as a resource centre for all departments.

At Reception and Key Stage 1 – and sometimes at Key Stage 2 – there will also be book corners or class libraries. And some secondary school English departments have book boxes from which students borrow for independent reading. These may be loaned to the department and changed regularly by the school library, or they may be a resource purchased by the English department. Ideally they offer a wide range of reading levels in fiction and non-fiction.

The purpose of all this is – obviously – to make as many

books available as possible to the pupils in order to encourage wider, faster, more committed reading.

As TA at Key Stages 1 and 2 you will probably have some responsibility for helping to manage the book stock. That could include:

- ordering books from catalogues and publishers
- collecting (and possibly choosing) books from the library
- maintaining the class book stock – tidying up, repairing books, etc.
- keeping in-class records of who has borrowed which book.

At Key Stage 1 you and the teacher need access to some 'Big Books'. These are a fairly recent development and several publishers produce them. Big Books are versions of ordinary books presented in a very large format – the size of an A2 tabloid newspaper like the *Daily Mail*. The idea is that you can sit down with a small group (or even a whole class) and everyone can see the pictures and some of the writing.

You will also probably:

- help the children to choose books in the classroom or in the school library
- escort small groups to the school library
- take small groups for activities based on the children's reading from the resource books.

Some schools also run bookshops or clubs through which books, often at discounted price or with profits to the school fund, are sold to children as another way of raising the profile of reading. You may find that part of your job is helping to run one of these.

You will find it easier to do any of these tasks if you are as familiar as possible with the books that you're handling – so it's back to the fact that reading promotes reading.

The public library

Many primary, and some secondary, schools take children to visit the public library as part of routine curriculum work. If the school you are in does not do this you might tactfully try to persuade the head or the teachers you're working with to think about it because it really does pay off.

The point is that many children do not come from families for whom library use is part of life, so they do not know what is inside the library and what it can offer. If children are taken there by the school by arrangement with the library staff, they meet the children's librarian, see the facilities and discover that there are – usually – many more books there than at school. Library staff are generally very happy to lay on an introductory session for groups of children from schools and to show them round the library. Many libraries run after-school and holiday events for children, and enthused pupils can then sometimes persuade their parents to bring them.

It's yet another way of getting children to regard reading as part of life by maximizing their exposure to books and introducing them to other adults who regard books as really important. The idea, remember, is to convert them from squiggle decoders into 'real readers'. You, as TA, could help to organize the library visit and go with the class on the day.

Reading in groups

There are several ways of sharing a book if you've got, say, four or six children in a group and you are all going to read the same book.

You can read part of it aloud while they follow and listen. Children can take it in turns to read small sections aloud, but never embarrass a child who finds reading aloud really difficult by insisting on it.

If you want the children to read the book independently, to enthuse them first you might:

- read aloud the opening, or the most exciting part, of the book as a 'taster'. Do not ask them to follow. They just need to listen and become involved
- ask them each to read the same chapter silently and then ask a few questions about it to start a discussion
- get a keen/able/'fast-lane' reader to read the book first in their own time a couple of weeks before. (This is a good 'extension' activity for a gifted and talented child.) The child introduces the book to the others by telling them just enough about it so that they want to read it too. Then all you have to do is produce the copies and invite them to leap in.

Incidentally, 'Open your books and climb in' is a silly catch phrase which has stood me in good stead for years (part of my 'book eccentric' image).

Film and DVD/video versions

Many children's books have been filmed for the cinema or TV and are now available as DVDs (or videos), for example: *The Chronicles of Narnia*, *The Railway Children*, *One Hundred and One Dalmatians*, *The Wind in the Willows*, *Mary Poppins*, *The Worst Witch*, *Watership Down* and many others. Sometimes it helps to show one of these to a group as a way of getting their interest, then you can introduce them to the book. A child who might struggle with a particular book 'cold' will often cope with it easily once he or she has seen a dramatization.

On the other hand, it also makes sense sometimes – with slightly abler readers – to tell them that you will let them see the film as a treat once the group has finished reading the book. Some will then be disappointed with the film, which cuts bits out and represents the characters differently from how the reader imagined, and you've made an important point – that reading is usually better.

Most children's films can be bought quite cheaply on DVD or, if the school has no budget for this, they can usually be borrowed for a small fee from the public library.

Can you make more use of book-linked films to encourage reading in your school?

Reading incentive schemes

Some schools are experimenting with points or reward schemes (a bit like supermarket loyalty schemes) to persuade pupils to read more books and to build up reading stamina.

The idea is that the more books a child reads the more points – or whatever – he or she gets. These then lead to some sort of reward, such as prizes, certificates or credit at the school bookshop. The difficulty is finding a way of checking that the books really have been read.

Accelerated Reader, part of Renaissance Learning (www.renaissance-learning.co.uk), is a way of making it easier for schools, and it's an example of such an idea in action. It's an American scheme, operating in 70,000 schools worldwide. More and more British schools seem to be signing up to it. Basically it's a computer program which includes carefully thought-out quizzes on thousands of books – from the simplest picture book through to long novels by Charles Dickens and Jane Austen. First, the pupil does a computerized test to find out what level he or she should be reading at and then borrows and reads a book with the right colour coding. Once the book is read the pupil does a computer quiz which checks that the book really has been read and understood. Only then can the pupil move on to another book. Children seem to enjoy doing this and in most participating schools they get rewards for reading more than a certain number of books or for progressing up a level.

The computer program doesn't cost much, but as Kathy Heaps, Headteacher of John Kelly Girls' Technology College in the London Borough of Brent – and a firm advocate of Accelerated Reader – says, 'The program is cheap but the students get so keen you have to buy a large numbers of books. I don't mind because it means that lots of reading is going on in my school.'

Schools which run Accelerated Reader – or other schemes similar to it – rely on TAs to help support the pupils as they choose and read their books and do their quizzes. It works best when there are several adults available to advise and help. Many TAs also find they are helping librarians and other staff to mobilize the book stock too.

Following book prizes

There are several prizes for children's books which are awarded annually – Smarties and Whitbread for example. Drawing young readers' attention to these, and encouraging them to read the shortlisted books before the winner is announced, is yet another way of keeping them interested in books.

The Carnegie Medal, for instance, has been awarded annually for a children's book since 1936. Past winners include *Pigeon Post* by Arthur Ransome, *The Borrowers* by Mary Norton, *The Owl Service* by Alan Garner and *Junk* by Melvyn Burgess. It is now run by the Chartered Institute of Library and Information Professionals (CILIP).

The judges are a large panel of children's librarians who announce their shortlist of five to eight books each April – chosen from books published between January and August the previous year. In recent years many schools have signed up to be Carnegie Medal shadowers. That means the children read the books, discuss them in their schools and post reviews on CILIP's website. CILIP provides advice and support materials for those wanting to take part.

When the winner is announced in June, pupils who have shadowed the prize take a real interest because they feel involved and have chosen their own winner – possibly the bookish equivalent of watching the fortunes of the football team you support.

This is something which a TA could do with a small group, or you could help to support a larger group if the teacher or librarian decides to lead Carnegie shadowing on a larger scale. The only resource needed is copies of the shortlisted books (see www.carnegiegreenaway.org.uk/shadowingsite).

Sponsored reading

Many pupils are motivated to read more if they know that their reading is also helping people in need. One way of making this happen is to hold a sponsored read. It works for any age group. You, the TA, could take responsibility for organizing it in one or more classes. You will need to:

- identify a charity that you all want to support
- decide whether to allow the pupils to read any book they choose or to have a set list – perhaps of titles the school has plenty of copies of
- fix on a time span – one week, two weeks or a month?
- think of a way of certifying that each book has been read – a parent or teacher to sign? Or you could set aside time in school, say every day for a month so that you can see that reading has been done. If you're really brave, have plenty of adults to help you and can do without sleep you could consider a 24-hour sponsored 'read-in' at a weekend
- devise the paperwork – sponsorship forms and checklists to record the list of books a child has read
- encourage the pupils to have as many sponsors as possible – the simplest way is to be sponsored so much per book. Alternatively the time spent reading can be sponsored at, say, 1p per minute – this is fiddly to monitor unless you say

nothing less than 20 minutes counts, but it can allow slower readers to take part on an equal basis

■ have a reasonably foolproof way of collecting the proceeds afterwards

■ take part yourself – and get your family and friends to sponsor you – so that it becomes a shared project.

Another possibility is to use Readathon (www.readathon.org) as the basis of your sponsored read. It is a charity which provides support for sponsored reading and raises funds for CLIC Sargent (www.clicsargent.org.uk) and the Roald Dahl Foundation (www.roalddahlfoundation.org).

Readathon, of which Roald Dahl was chairman from 1988 until his death in 1990, was started in 1984 to encourage reading. The money it raises helps children with cancer, Hodgkin's disease, leukaemia, epilepsy, blood disorders and acquired brain injury. Although it is ideal for Children's Book Week in October – when many schools run a sort of literacy festival – you can do Readathon at any time of the year.

It supplies a free pack containing:

■ sponsor forms
■ badges, stickers and other extras for participants
■ literacy-based project materials
■ coloured posters
■ organizer's guidelines.

Authors visiting schools

Many children's authors visit schools to talk to pupils about the books they've written and to encourage children with their literacy. Many will spend a whole day in a school, working with different groups.

Children get very excited about meeting authors and it is a powerful way of encouraging reading. Pupils will want to read some of the books before they meet a writer. Or, if the author visit comes first, they are motivated and curious to read the books afterwards. Most authors bring copies of their books with them so that pupils – advised in advance to bring some money – can buy them and get them signed. (You could invite parents and let them do the buying.) Authors will usually sign copies of their books already owned by pupils or the school.

This can be time consuming for a busy class teacher to set up, so it could be something which you, the TA, might offer to do. You can approach writers by writing to the publisher which produces their books. (Publisher contact details are printed at the front of all books.) The National Association of Writers in Education (www.nawe.co.uk) has a directory on its website of authors who make school visits. The Society of Authors may also be able to help (www.societyofauthors.net). Another useful website is www.contactanauthor.co.uk, and the Literacy Trust has helpful advice about authors in schools on its website www.literacytrust.org.uk/

As self-employed people, authors visiting schools do, of course, have to charge for their time, so if this isn't part of your school budget you have to find a way of paying for it. The school's Friends Association or Parent Teacher Association (PTA) might help for instance, or there might be a local business which would sponsor it.

You can sometimes get help through Arts Councils which have some funds to support this sort of work:

- England: www.artscouncil.org.uk
- Northern Ireland: www.artscouncil-ni.org
- Scotland: Scottish Arts Council: www.scottisharts.org.uk
- Wales: Arts Council of Wales: www.artswales.org.uk/

And when you've got it organized don't forget to invite the local paper to come and take some pictures. Author visits are quite high profile and it will be a feather in your cap with the headteacher if you can get some good, positive publicity for the school. And it could be yet another literacy activity to read with the children what the local paper wrote about them.

Lovereading4schools

Lovereading is a basically an online bookshop, but it is also doing some quite interesting things to help develop children into real readers. There are three websites: for grownups there is www.lovereading.co.uk

Children are well catered for at www.lovereading4kids.co.uk where they can download and read the opening chapters of books they're interested in. There are also lots of book recommendations by children for children, aimed at all age ranges. Author of the month is a regular feature. And then there is www.lovereading4schools.co.uk, which has useful reading lists for Years 1–9, along with lots of information about books. Parents can register too, so that they find out about the books which the school is recommending.

Encouraging children to use some of the material on the sites could:

- introduce them and you to books and authors which are new to you
- be in itself part of literacy work because the material on the sites has to be read
- create writing opportunities for children who want to submit reviews
- link with ICT work.

What use could you make of these sites to help develop literacy in your school?

Traditional comprehension exercises

Before we leave the subject of extending and developing reading ability, stamina and interest, I have to mention old-fashioned comprehension exercises. I mean that read-the-passage-and-answer-the-ten-questions work which you may remember from your own schooldays.

The word 'comprehension' means understanding or taking in. So it's a key strand of literacy. Think back – sometimes reading that passage at school encouraged us to look in the library for the book so that we could read the rest of it. There is still plenty of scope for this.

Now, the approach is usually a bit different. Yes, of course literacy teachers still try to develop comprehension skills. But consider this example:

Statement in extract: Fred sat down and ate his falafel.
Question: What did Fred eat?
Answer: He ate a falafel.

Most educators now think this is a bit pointless because you can answer correctly without having the faintest idea what a falafel is, so it doesn't really have much to do with real comprehension or understanding! (A falafel, by the way, is a spicy lentil cake popular in Arabic countries such as Egypt.) Although this is an absurdly simple example to make the point clear, a lot of slightly more complicated, traditional comprehension exercises worked in exactly this way.

Passages and extracts offered at all levels to children in, for example, National Curriculum tests tend now to be used in a rather more sophisticated way. A child might now be asked, for instance, to sum up in his own words what a character in the passage thinks about something or to list three reasons for something that has happened.

So, you need to be aware of this as you work with children on comprehension passages – or even help to devise them. Deal with straightforward things like what a specific word means by talking about it, then get the children to do slightly more challenging tasks in writing.

And, most importantly, remember that every passage a child reads has the potential to be a stimulus for wider reading. Encourage the child to read the book (or newspaper, magazine or whatever) that it came from.

Doing the job

Lindsay Barton, mother of four, has worked at New Oscott, one of the largest primary schools in Birmingham, for 11 years. She was attached to the infant department before it merged with the juniors in 2005.

I work in Year 3 with special needs children. I do a lot of one-to-one helping to identify words and letters through a wide range of activities and games. I also do guided reading with children in groups of six to eight at all levels, including poetry and its techniques for those who can manage it.

We don't use a specific reading scheme. Instead we have a large number of colour-coded books from which children practise reading. And that's in addition to classroom book corners and the school library. Every class spends time in the library every week and I help the children choose books. The library is open after school too so that parents can come in. Every child has a library ticket and, of course, books can be taken home. We also run book weeks to encourage the buying of books. A private company works with us on this.

I also help with 'paired reading'. This is a scheme in which an older child – usually one who is a slow reader compared with the rest of his or her usual group – 'helps' a younger child. We do quite a lot of this with Year 5/Year 2 pairings. You have to pick the children carefully, but if you get it right it is excellent for the confidence of the older child. It also brings on the younger one.

Either a teacher or a TA reads aloud to every class every day and we swap classes for this so that the children get a variety.

I help children to prepare drama for assemblies. That often means learning lines which is a useful literacy activity. We also do a lot of book-based role-play in drama. It encourages the children to read and to know the plot of the story because acting it out brings the book to life.

6

Speaking and listening

Children listen before they speak. A newborn baby hears the sounds which other people make – and a lot of it is words. There is now evidence that babies hear sounds and begin to process them while still in the womb.

Gurgles, coos and shrieks are very gradually shaped into imitations of the words that the child hears. A child who cannot hear or who can hear only partially, of course, does not begin to speak in the usual way and needs specialist help. So listening and speaking are really two sides of the same coin.

Children speak before they read or write. A command of spoken language is an essential forerunner of reading. Research shows too that children need spoken language in order to be able to think and reason. Without words, some experts say, actions are instinctive like an animal's are – not thought out – although a child, as any parent knows, understands quite complex word sequences long before he or she can say them. It is language and the elaborate communication it allows, of course, which distinguishes humans from animals.

So children need to be able to listen and speak as well as possible before they can begin to learn to read formally. If they are late learning to read it could be that they still need help with their pre-reading language skills, and that means plenty of oral work.

In the world of work and everyday human life communication is about 80 per cent oral (and only 20 per cent written). That is another reason why we need to develop children's listening and speaking skills to the highest possible level through the years at school as an ongoing part of their literacy work. And you, the TA, have a big part to play in this.

Speaking and listening is now part of the assessment of children's English and literacy in the tests at Key Stages 1, 2 and 3. It is also part (about 20 per cent of the marks) of GCSE English.

None of this, incidentally, is anything to do with elocution, 'talking posh' or 'the rain in Spain'. The modern emphasis in speaking and listening is on strong, lively communication – not Buckingham Palace diction.

The chance to talk

If you want youngsters to learn to talk effectively you have to let them do it. No skill improves without practice. And if that sounds too obvious to say I make no apology for mentioning it because it often isn't understood. If you are constantly shutting children up, they cannot learn to talk well. 'Being seen and not heard', as the Victorians recommended, will not produce articulate speakers.

Traditionally children worked very quietly in schools – often, indeed, in silence with punishments for speaking. And much as you and your colleagues might sometimes long for a few minutes of that quiet, pupils do need plenty of opportunity to talk, both informally among themselves and more formally with adults, if they are to grow into good oral communicators. And that applies at all stages of their education.

That does not mean, of course, that there will not also be times when the children should work quietly. It is a question of balance and of valuing spoken literacy as an integral part of the bigger picture of literacy.

Think about how you can get the children in your school to speak more confidently.

Open questions

If you are trying to encourage children of any age to speak expansively then it is no good asking them closed questions. 'Closed' questions can be dismissed with a very brief answer.

If you ask, 'Did you enjoy your lunch?' a child who doesn't feel like being forthcoming, or who is shy or lacking in confidence will simply say 'Yes' (or 'No') and the conversation grinds to an immediate halt. Similarly the question, 'Who brought you to school today?' invites the answer, 'Mum' (or 'Dad' or 'My brother'). 'How many sisters have you got? ('Two', 'Three', 'None') doesn't get a discussion started either.

So, in order to develop children's oral skills, you need to be aware of the importance of 'open' questions which encourage the child to answer more fully. Open questions are 'open' to a full answer.

Some examples of open questions for different age levels are:

- What did you have for lunch today?
- Tell me about your journey to school?
- What does your Teddy think about it?
- What is your book about?
- What did you do at playtime?
- How did you spend the lunch break?
- Tell me about your family?

Useful phrases for open questions include:

- What do you think about . . . ?
- How do you . . . ?
- Tell me/your partner/the group about . . . ?
- Can you explain why . . . ?
- Can you describe . . . ?
- I'd love to know what you think about . . . ?

Be careful not to ask a question and answer it in the same breath before the child has had time to think about it. Don't say, 'I bet you don't like the way the classroom's been painted during the holidays because you hate that colour, don't you?' Say, 'What do you think of the new decorations?' Don't say (to a Muslim or Jewish child), 'You don't have Christmas do you?' Say, 'What interesting things does your family do during the Christmas holidays?'

From Key Stage 2 onwards talk to the children about open questions too. Train them to use them in pair and group work when they are speaking to each other.

 Make your own list of useful open questions. It will help you to get into the habit of thinking about them and using them.

Circle time

Circle time is an idea used a lot in primary schools from the nursery class to Year 6. Increasingly it is also used at Key Stage 3, often as part of tutor group sessions or in personal, social and health education (PSHE) lessons.

It involves the children sitting in a ring on the floor or on chairs with one or more adults – without desks and tables because they create barriers. As TA you sit in the circle as an equal, not a superior. The children take it turns to tell the group about a piece of news or about something which is, for example, worrying/exciting/interesting them. The rest know they must listen to each other, not interrupt, and ask interested follow-up questions.

Some teachers provide an object that can be passed around the circle with only the person holding it being allowed to speak at any time. This object could be anything – a toy, perhaps, or a natural object such as a large shell – as long as it is bulky enough for the rest of the circle to see clearly who is holding it. Each person should be able to see everyone's face too.

If you are new to circle time the framework set out by expert Barbara Maines might be helpful:

- Circle time is a space within the school curriculum into which each person comes with unconditional acceptance.
- It is not the place for judgement or coercion.
- It provides an opportunity to learn and explore through the discussion of experiences and individuality.

Circle time is an opportunity for children to learn the skills they need to thrive in life, such as effective communication, emotional literacy, anger management, peer mediation and conflict resolution. These may, in turn, help to improve behaviour, but this is a side-effect rather than a goal.

Circle time develops pupils' speaking and listening skills, but it is not simply a space in which to moan. It is a positive activity. If things get negative then you and the teacher should try to get the children to look for positive solutions or outcomes.

To start the circle time process you and/or the teacher might:

- organize a quick game to get pupils trusting one another and cooperating. This is all good groundwork for facilitating useful discussions
- introduce a whole group ice breaker such as a guessing game
- encourage discussion of likes and dislikes, or personal goals and wishes
- get discussions going under the title: 'best day, worst day'. Be prepared for some potentially revealing thoughts from pupils
- use song, music, story, rhythm, chants, dance, mime, and so on. The aims of circle time can be achieved in many ways.

Circle time needs to follow a recognizable pattern. For example:

1   An opening activity, rounds (such as asking every member of the circle what their favourite food is or, for more complex responses, asking each person what they would do if, say, they witnessed a child being bullied)
2   Brainstorming for the class (for example, blasting out ideas for your end-of-year celebrations), or discussion (on a key topic of the moment)
3   Closure activity.

However many component parts you and the teacher decide to adopt, stick to that as the overall plan. Be aware that children sometimes mention delicate or confidential things in circle time. These need handling sensitively. You as TA, may find yourself fielding cultural issues too – some children from some backgrounds are not very comfortable about speaking out.

Not everyone needs to participate in every discussion or round. It's fine for pupils to 'pass' if they need or want to, as long as they don't avoid all participation. Circle time is a good space in which to spot withdrawn behaviour. Watch out for those who try to dominate proceedings too. As TA you are able to have a word or find other tactful ways of helping.

Try to enjoy circle time with the children and the teacher. Your enthusiasm, participation and appreciation of the pupils' contributions can really help to make it work well.

A number of useful books have been written about circle time, especially by Jenny Mosley and Charlie Smith. Some of these are listed in Chapter 8.

Think about circle time in your own school and how it is used (if it is). What do the children you work with gain from it?

Speaking and listening activities with small groups

Much of the oral work you can do with children whose literacy is developing is an extension of what might be done with pre-literate pupils as discussed in Chapter 2. They still need singing and rhymes, especially at Key Stages 1 and 2. Just make the songs and rhymes slightly less babyish. Go to a children's poetry book rather than a nursery rhyme book, for example.

The adaptable ideas listed here will work for various age or ability levels.

- Play 'I went to Tesco and I bought . . .' The first child says, for example, 'I went to Tesco and I bought a cabbage.' The second repeats the opening statement and adds something of his own. So it becomes, 'I went to Tesco and I bought a cabbage and a toothbrush.' As you go round the group more and more items get listed. This is good for making the children listen and concentrate. You can 'sex' this up for Key Stage 3 pupils by making it a more exciting shop if you wish. With an older or advanced group it is fun, and adds another literacy dimension, to do this with book titles: 'I went to Amazon.co.uk (or Waterstones) and bought *Harry Potter and the Half-Blood Prince*, *The Railway Children*, *The Very Hungry Caterpillar* and . . .' (Key Stages 1, 2 and 3).

- One child chooses an object and describes it without naming it. The others have to guess what he or she is describing. So the lead child might say that the object is a rectangular space in a wall with glass in it (window) or a cylindrical, hollow object with a handle for drinking from (mug) or a spherical object thrown, hit, kicked or caught for sport (ball). This is a good way of getting children to listen. It is also excellent for encouraging a child to use carefully chosen vocabulary. Don't allow gestures, the rule is words only. You can devise a points system and have rules about asking and answering questions or giving clues if you wish (Key Stages 2 and 3).

■ The group makes up a story by taking it in turns to add a sentence. The first might say, 'Once there was a girl who lived in Manchester.' The next might add, 'Her name was Elena.' The third might say, 'One day she and her mother went into the city on the bus to visit her aunt.' And so on. This usually gets silly in the end and causes a lot of (healthy) laughter. As well as getting children to make oral contributions, it helps them to get a feel for what a sentence is (Key Stage 2 or 3).

■ Tell a story word by word. Go round the group, each person adding a word. So the first child says 'Jon', the second 'went', the third 'to', and so on. Keep it slick and the results can be hilarious. This is the sort of activity which works much better in a small group than in a whole class because no one has to wait long between turns (Key Stages 2 or 3).

■ Each child in the group talks for 30 seconds about something they like to do – get them to prepare this in advance. They can have notes but should not read what they want to say (Key Stages 2 and 3).

■ Children take it in turns to tell the others in the group about a book they have read and enjoyed (Key Stages 1, 2 and 3).

■ Give the group a picture (clipped from a magazine or newspaper) in which it is not clear what is really happening. The children can then talk about it and make up a story together to explain what is going on in the picture. It is worth looking out for suitably enigmatic pictures and keeping them ready in a folder (Key Stages 1, 2 and 3).

■ You set a problem and get the children to work out the answer by talking about it – for example, there are four people in a balloon (a mother of four young children, a man of 70 who is close to discovering a cure for all types of cancer, a brilliant teacher aged 28 and a very rich woman aged 30, who regularly gives large sums to famine relief). The children could help invent the characters. The balloon is losing height. All will die unless one person jumps out to lighten the load. Get the children to talk about which one of the four it should be (Key Stages 2 and 3).

- Each child prepares – by practising at home or with you in a quiet moment – a paragraph from a book or a short poem to read aloud to the group (Key Stages 1, 2 and 3).
- Group role-play. Think (helped by the children) of a situation such a family meal. One of the group is the father, another a visiting uncle, a third a teenage girl and so on. Something has happened (one of the children is in trouble with the police?). Work out the conversation. The skill is to think of a plausible situation for the group size that you're working with (Key Stages 1, 2 and 3).
- Play 'Just A Minute', as on BBC Radio 4. You give an individual pupil a subject (cats, school dinners, roadworks or whatever). The child has to talk for one minute on the topic without hesitation, deviation or repetition. If they pause, deviate or repeat anything one of the other children challenges and then takes over the subject until the minute is up (Key Stage 3, ideal for a gifted and talented group).
- Play 'Call My Bluff'. One group of three children presents an unfamiliar word found in the dictionary (for example, holm, roux or tinea) to the rest of the group. They then offer three meanings, one each, and the others have to guess – or work out – which definition is the right one. For tinea, for instance, they might say it's a South American rat, a fungal skin disease and a carpenter's tool (it is a fungal disease). They will talk together usefully and learn a lot by looking through the dictionary for the words. Making up the definitions is a useful literacy task too. The more detail each definition adds, the more fun it gets (Key Stage 3, ideal for a gifted and talented group).

Talk – supported by its close relation, listening – can be used for many purposes including, for example, to establish social contact, to narrate, describe, explain, negotiate, perform and to try out, or work out, ideas. The activities suggested above range across all of these and you will soon think of others.

Play some of the games above with your groups. Listen to the children carefully. Can you work out what particular individuals are learning?

Using talk as you support individuals

When you, as TA, are working one-to-one within a class there are good opportunities to develop the speaking and listening part of literacy. And this applies just as much in, say, a science, design technology or RE lesson as it does in English.

If a pupil is trying to answer questions on a worksheet, but struggling to find the answers, don't simply tell them what to write. Ask questions which will lead the pupil towards the answer. Each time you ask a question and insist that the pupil replies you are discussing the problem in a constructive way. The child is both listening and speaking.

For example, suppose a Year 5 child is having difficulty with work on the nine times table and is stuck over 6×9. Don't just tell her that it's 54. Ask her what 5×9 or 7×9 is and suggest adding or subtracting 9. Ask what 3×9 is. Then you can double it. Ask what 12×9 is then you can halve it. Ask the child if she can think of a way of working out the answers and, having found the answer, can she think of a way of remembering it?

Question and show rather than tell is a principle of a lot of teaching. It is particularly effective as a means of developing literacy.

Subject-based vocabulary

As children learn all the different curriculum subjects and the timetable becomes more specialized as they progress through Key Stage 2 towards Key Stage 3, they will learn specific words for every subject. For example:

English: noun, phoneme, exclamation mark
Mathematics: subtract, hexagon, factor
Science: hypothesis, pancreas, test tube
Geography: valley, silt, agriculture
Modern foreign language: gender, accent, infinitive
Art: impressionism, texture, palate
Music: crescendo, oboe, synthesizer
History: source, reign, revolt
RE: worship, culture, respect
PE: vault, javelin, backstroke
ICT: byte, pixel, email
DT: acrylic, textile, temperature.

Children need to be as fluent as possible in this specialist vocabulary from as early an age as possible. That means a lot of conversation with each other and with adults like you in which the words are used accurately and naturally. Most children will not be able to absorb such words properly into their written work until they are confident and comfortable with them orally.

Be aware, too, that children are sometimes confused by words which change their meaning depending on which subject is being learned and taught. For example, the word volume means:

- solid space in mathematics or science. You might measure the volume of a cube or cylinder.
- a book in English or in the library. 'Look in the third volume of the encyclopedia.'

- the level of sound in music. 'Turn down the bass volume on the electronic keyboard.'

Other 'chameleon words' include:

- beat (in sport, cookery, music)
- tap (tap root, tap dance, gas tap, phone tap, threads on screws in DT)
- set (set square, sorting sets in mathematics, sets in tennis, set book)

Every day in schools hundreds of these words which shift their meanings continually are used. Most children pick most of them up as they go along, but some have difficulty. Be alert to this.

 Think about language and how it is used in different subjects. You will be able to add lots of examples to the ones listed here.

SEN groups

Children in mainstream schools with SEN are likely to have short concentration spans. This can make problems if you are trying to do speaking and listening work in small groups. A child who loses interest is likely to distract the others and then the activity can flounder. So:

- change the activity/game/task every few minutes
- don't ask children to sit in the same place for too long
- put different sorts of activities in the same lesson
- alternate written activities with speaking and listening work
- if the children are working in pairs, think carefully about which children work together.

Children on the autistic spectrum often find speaking and listening the hardest part of literacy. Communication difficulties are often part of the disability. They may well need specialist help and/or you may need specialist training to learn how best to help them.

On the other hand, dyslexic children who find written work so difficult may be quite competent as speakers and listeners. In fact, this is an area where they might shine, so it's a good opportunity to raise their self-esteem. That means plenty of encouragement and praise from you.

English Speaking Board

The English Speaking Board (ESB), now an international organization, was founded in 1953 to encourage good oral communication. Its main activity is to examine children (and adults) in speaking and listening and to make awards for oral achievement.

At Key Stages 1, 2 and 3 this means that a group of children works with an adult – a teacher or TA, or both. Over several months each child prepares a talk about a hobby or interest. Then comes the day when the ESB examiner arrives. It's a group activity. The pupils deliver their prepared talks and each answers questions on the topic of the talk from the rest of the group. Reading aloud and chatting to the examiner is also part of the test. At the end of the day each child gets a certificate at one of three levels.

This is a very good way of raising the status of speaking and listening in a school. And preparing children for an ESB exam is something a TA could do, either as a weekly session or as an out-of-school activity. The problem is that there is a small cost to the school because there is an entrance fee for each child. This pays for the examiner and means that the school benefits from ESB advice and materials. That is why ESB activities are commoner in fee-paying schools than in state ones. But the system does operate in some state schools (in every school in

Guernsey, for example, where the local education authority pays the fee).

There are various ways of funding entrance fees which different schools have tried:

- invite the parents to make a contribution
- budget to pay for it out of the school's resources
- get sponsorship from a local business
- from time to time ESB itself gets some sponsorship centrally which it can use to help state schools.

The work of ESB is not as well known as it should be. Perhaps you could talk to the headteacher and to teachers in your school about it. If you take responsibility for it, the work could benefit your learning as well as the children's. There is a lot more information on ESB's website: www.esbuk.org/

Doing the job

Shirley Peek has worked at Collingwood Primary School in South Woodham Ferrers, Essex, for 16 years, first as a volunteer when her children were pupils, then as a dinner lady and now as a TA.

I first became a TA because the school needed someone to work one-to-one on literacy with a child with a statement of special needs. She had speech and language problems so the work was very specific.

I did a course on special needs to learn how to do this work and how best to help the child because I was completely new to it. In school I worked closely with the visiting speech therapist. She saw 'my' child regularly and then recommended what she and I needed to do until the therapist's next visit. I also worked with the child's mother to make sure she got ongoing back-up support at home. So it was a three-way partnership to help her. I went on doing this work at all levels until the child transferred to secondary school.

Now I'm based in Years 5 and 6. None of the children have statements but there are ten with individual education plans (IEPs). Generally I sit at a table in the classroom with them while the teacher is at the front. It's better to keep them in the same room so that they feel they belong, rather than with-drawing them too often. A lot of what I do with them is about helping them to listen well and to speak with more confidence so that they meet their individual targets. Some older boys are inclined to 'switch off' but I find they will usually ask me for help when they need it.

7

Wider literacy

Literacy goes a long way beyond the narrowness of the traditional four strands of the English curriculum – reading, writing, speaking and listening – which we have looked at in the earlier chapters of this book.

It is part of every other subject on the curriculum. As well as being the blood and bones of English, literacy is also an essential part of these subjects, all of which are compulsory for under-14s attending state schools:

- Mathematics
- Science
- Information and communications technology (ICT)
- Design technology
- History
- Geography
- Music
- Art and design
- Physical education (PE)
- Modern foreign language (usually French or Spanish)
- Religious education (RE) (parents may withdraw their children)
- Personal, social and health education (parents may withdraw their children from sex education)
- Citizenship.

Examples of literacy work in other subjects

If you are supporting an individual child you will have to help him or her learn in a range of subjects, not just in lessons which are designated 'literacy' or English. But literacy will underpin the work. For example:

- In a Key Stage 1 science lesson a child might need help with reading or writing labels, perhaps the parts of the body or the names of the planets. Help might also be needed with basic science words such as 'experiment' and 'evidence'.

- Citizenship at all levels often involves reading the news in newspapers and on websites. The child or group you are working with may need guidance and support to access the information they need.

- Much music is made in groups. In order to work with others you have to discuss ideas. This too is part of literacy and you, as TA, may need to join in discussions to show the children how to use talk to reach useful conclusions.

- If a history lesson requires a Year 6 pupil to describe, say, a Victorian home he might need help with planning, organizing and setting out the writing.

- When children are learning ICT there are always instructions to be read on-screen. They may need help both with reading and interpreting these, especially at Key Stage 1.

The higher a pupil's standard of literacy the higher their achievements in all other subjects are likely to be. So it's important to keep chipping away at it.

It often helps a child to be doing literacy work via another subject anyway. For a child who is behind most of the others in the class, being made to do (seemingly) endless extra work on 'literacy' can be boring and demoralizing. If the literacy work is disguised because the pupil is actually doing geography or art, then it can be a good opportunity for extra literacy without the pupil being too aware of it. Think of it as literacy by the painless drip-feed method.

 Take a few minutes to reflect on how literacy is essential to other subjects. Do it as a cross-referencing exercise. Are there any subjects which do not depend on literacy?

Role of drama and poetry

Most children and young people love drama and it can be a real help with literacy because:

- it builds confidence
- it provides speaking and listening opportunities
- drama scripts are usually written
- pupils usually enjoy it so they are motivated to read and write anything required by the drama activity they are engaged in
- it can be a spontaneous form of expression (in role-play, for instance).

Poetry can be:

- funny
- moving
- thoughtful
- dramatic
- entertaining
- quirky.

A child who is daunted by a book, or even a short story, can often be persuaded to read and enjoy a poem because it is short. Read poems aloud to children as often as you can to get their interest. It's also a useful time filler if you've got a minute or two left before the bell.

As TA, encourage all the pupils you work with to take part

in as much drama as possible. And don't be afraid to bring drama into other subjects. If it helps with a bit of mathematics for each child to pretend to be a number, then do it. If it's difficult to understand what happened when Henry VIII wanted to marry Anne Boleyn, act it out as a little play.

And make sure you know plenty of poems and have some good poetry books handy. *The New Dragon Book of Verse* and *The Young Dragon Book of Verse* are good stand-bys – both published by Oxford University Press. Children, even if they are academically quite limited, often like writing poetry too. Encourage it. It is all part of building up literacy.

You can often link poetry and drama together. Many good poems (such as 'The Highwayman' by Alfred Noyes, 'Timothy Winters' by Charles Causley or 'We are Seven' by William Wordsworth) tell stories. So encourage the pupils to act them out using words and movement.

 Think about how you can use poetry to help the literacy of the pupils you work with.

Literacy activities across the curriculum

In any curriculum lesson a child might be helped with literacy by:

- playing an oral game which uses language (for example, in geography think of a river for each letter of the alphabet – Amazon, Brahmaputra, Cam, Danube . . . Or, in science, pretend to be a famous scientist such as Isaac Newton or Marie Curie, while the others guess who you are)
- writing emails (for example, to children in other countries as part of citizenship or RE, or to invite visitors to the school as part of PSHE)
- writing letters (for example, to newspapers or to thank people who have helped the school or class)

- reading instructions
- consulting encyclopaedias, reference books or the Internet to get specific information
- leading, or taking part in, a debate
- introducing a speaker in class or an assembly
- introducing something to a group such a music performance or piece of art
- explaining their design in DT to someone else
- reading books which tell them more about a curriculum subject (for example, the novel *The White Darkness* by Geraldine McCaughrean to learn about Antarctica).

As TA you need to be aware of the value to children's literacy of such activities and do what you can to promote them.

External literacy projects

Because of the cross-curricular links between literacy and other subjects, many organizations run, or help to run, education projects in schools which are designed to develop literacy as well as other learning. In fact, if a project is meant for 5–11-year-olds it really has to be literacy driven these days or schools will say they don't have time to fit it in.

These projects come from theatre companies, art galleries, businesses such as banks, charities, museums, organizations such as The National Trust and English Heritage, higher education institutions, partnerships between independent schools and state schools, newspapers and many others.

As TA you might:

- find yourself working with such a project because the headteacher and teaching staff have arranged for it to operate in your school or with pupils from your school. See it as a good learning opportunity for yourself
- hear of an opportunity and bring it to the attention of the school's management team and then take some or all of the

responsibility for organizing the visit or whatever the project involves

- afterwards, use ideas which have come from the project with your small group or with pupils you are individually supporting.

Examples of external literacy projects

Can I have a word?

In 2006 the Barbican's Education Department started an ongoing poetry-based literacy project called Can I have a word? for nine- and ten-year-olds.

It involves poets and writers such as Michael Rosen, Matthew Sweeney, Beverley Naidoo and Debjani Chatterjee. They work at the Barbican Centre in the City of London with children from ten London primary schools in Islington, Tower Hamlets and the City. Neither the schools nor the parents have to pay.

For example, Year 5 children from John Scurr Primary School, Bethnal Green, went to the Barbican with their teachers and TAs and watched a film called *The Red Balloon*. Then the poet Rena Edwards helped them to write about what they'd seen from different points of view.

Lots of words and phrases were displayed around the room. Poetry was shown as something that anyone can do. Before long the pupils were each writing a poem of their own and 'performing' their work on stage in front of the rest of the group.

Poets and Barbican education staff have run training sessions for the participating teachers and TAs to help them to get the best out of the project for their children.

Back at John Scurr School displays relating to the children's Barbican work went on the wall. Children also read their poems aloud in assembly and invited parents to hear them.

Any TA or teacher can download free the resources, discussions, poems and short videos that this project uses: www.barbican.org.uk/canihaveaword/ TAs could research this for the children and classes they work with. There are four sets of themed teaching ideas based on *The Odyssey*, the human body, changing voices and the elements.

Wider teaching suggestions include showing ways of linking *The Odyssey* to the national curriculum for history – pupils can learn about ancient Greek life, the alphabet and the Olympic Games. Or you can link Matthew Sweeney's poem 'Water' with science.

A TA taking a whole class for literacy work in the absence of the teacher might find such resources particularly useful.

Sugar and slate

In 2005 schools in the quarrying district of Bethesda in North Wales undertook a literacy project coordinated by the University of Wales, Bangor. It took four afternoons and the idea, at schools such as Llanllechid Primary, was to get the children to focus on words and literacy while also learning about the history of their area – slate quarrying and the sugar cane tended by slaves in the West Indies which financed it.

Lesson plans, which TAs helped to devise, looked something like this:

Afternoon 1

1   How to introduce yourself – by reflecting on what makes you different from everyone else in the class. Each pupil to write an introduction about her/himself and to write a description of a partner. Aim of activity: a) to recognize that each child is different, before going on to look at children from a different country, b) to identify the difference between primary and secondary research. The partners writing about each other have missed out some important points. Likewise with finding out about people from another country, it's best to ask them about themselves directly rather than to read what others have written about them. Introduce the idea of a class email.

2   Start the email – each individual introduces themselves.
3   Pupils describe the place they live in under general headings, such as environment, view, leisure activity, etc. Include a general description of their area in the email.
4   Awareness mapping of what pupils already know, or think they know, about Jamaica. Pupils then consider what they don't know but would like to know, and add their questions to the email. Send.

Afternoon 2
1   Poems by Jamaicans, including British Jamaicans such as Benjamin Zephaniah.
2   *Bullies and Blacklegs* – a novel by Brenda Wyn Jones about the strike in the slate quarry owned by Lord Penrhyn (the same dynasty that profited from slavery and sugar in Jamaica and opposed abolition).
3   Write a bubble script – for first chapter to be taped and reviewed.
4   Mind-mapping about Jamaica, with pictures.

Afternoon 3
1   Formal script – developing and formalizing the ideas developed in the bubble script.
2   Tape – using script.
3   Fruit – experience of tropical fruit using smell, taste, touch, sight, sound.
4   Learning a song such as 'Mango Walk', 'Liza', 'Freedom'.

Afternoon 4
1   Brenda Wyn Jones – author visit providing background to her novel and an introduction to the process of writing and book production.
2   Class discussion/evaluation of the success of project. 'What have we learned?'
3   Summary of evaluation on a PowerPoint presentation.

In connection with a project like this a TA might:

- pool ideas with teachers and TAs at the planning stage
- meet staff from the coordinating university and/or other schools alongside teachers
- prepare resources
- help the children with specific tasks
- keep an eye on any child likely to need help
- organize the author visit.

Wordscapes

Renaissance is a national scheme to transform England's regional museums. It provides alternative learning approaches to literacy for pupils aged 5–16. Under this umbrella, schools and museums in the east of England have devised Wordscapes – workshops which use museum artefacts to help children with the literacy curriculum.

After looking at paintings in the museum galleries Key Stage 1 and 2 children make ingenious 'wordholders' to contain their newly created 'wordscape'. In other words, pupils look at, say, a painting, collect new words and turn them into writing. The Key Stage 1 poetry activity, for example, invites the children to edit/change/turn upside down. The children enjoy making their own words and not having to make the poem rhyme or fit into a format.

At the Fitzwilliam Museum in Cambridge the education staff are also delivering project days for pupils at Key Stage 3. The project brings together education staff from eight museums including Kettles Yard, The University Museum of Classical Archaeology, The Sedgwick Museum of Earth Sciences, the Cecil Higgins Art Gallery in Bedford and Peterborough Museum, along with a literacy adviser from Bedford.

A TA in a participating school might:

- attend training sessions run by museum staff
- work and learn alongside the children they are helping

during sessions (one of the joys of working in education is that you never stop exploring areas which are new to you)

■ help children to think of new words and introduce them to words they don't know

■ support SEN children to ensure they have the same opportunities as other pupils.

Consider any external projects your school has taken part in. How did the children's literacy benefit?

Doing the job

Sue Smith is a TA at Greenacre, a boys' high school in Chatham, Medway, Kent. She has been there for four years, having previously been a primary school TA for seven years.

If you are working with 'challenging' pupils it is very important to find topics and projects which really interest them. Then you can use that as a way of getting into literacy. Many really need an alternative curriculum. Football is often a good starting point. It gives you and the pupil something to discuss, read and write about. I use open questions to get them communicating.

Some of the pupils I work with are doing practical work in subjects like horticulture or garden-making. That's useful for literacy too. You can use their experience and then relate it to literacy work. It helps them to see a point in what you are trying to get them to do.

When I'm supporting in the classroom I listen to the teacher in an exaggerated manner so that the pupils see me doing it.

Role-modelling is a really good tool. Then I praise the pupils for listening. And when I was a TA in a primary school we used to have a Literacy Star of the Day – a little honour awarded on a points system to the child who had demonstrated the best listening and concentration on work.

I did a day-release course at the local further and higher education college, accredited by South Bank University. It has given me 120 points towards a degree. The school has a 'literacy drive' and a cross-curricular policy and the course was very relevant. I am going to apply for a Higher Level Teaching Assistant (HLTA) post at Greenacre.

I think it's very important that new TAs get proper induction. There are so many acronyms and so much jargon in education and EBD (emotional and behavioural difficulties) work. Without a bit of training at the beginning you probably wouldn't know what your colleagues were talking about.

8

More resources

Further background information about literacy

Foundations of Literacy by Sue Palmer and Ros Bayley, Network Educational Press (2004, revised 2005)

Early Literacy Work with Families by Cathy Nutbrown, Peter Hannon and Anne Morgan, Sage (2005)

Just Playing? The role and status of play in early childhood education by Janet R. Moyles, Open University Press (1989)

Supporting Writing by Sylvia Edwards, David Fulton Publishers (2004)

Supporting Speaking and Listening by Angela Wilson, David Fulton Publishers (2004)

The Curious Incident of the Dog in the Night-time by Mark Haddon, Vintage (2003) (a novel which gives real insight into autism)

Reception and Key Stage 1 resources

Video and DVD theme packs to encourage role play at Foundation Stage and Key Stage 1, Early Vision Tel: 01989 567353 Web: www.earlyvision.co.uk

Quicksilver Theatre company has a bookable show which it takes to schools and other settings. *Upstairs in the Sky* by Carey English and Guy Holland is about children playing. At the end the children in the audience join in by playing with the items which make up the set. Quicksilver Theatre, 4 Enfield Road London N1 5AZ Tel: 020 7241 2942 Web: www.quicksilvertheatre.org

Sue Palmer's Synthetic Phonix – www.philipandtacey.co.uk

www.bbc.co.uk/schools/wordsandpictures

Superphonics (Books 1–5) by Ruth Miskin, Hodder Children's Books

Jolly Phonics – www.jollylearning.co.uk

Living Phonics – www.ransom.co.uk

Storyworlds – www.heinemann.co.uk

Here We Go Round: Quality Circle Time for 3–5 year olds by Jenny Mosley, Positive Press Ltd (2005)

Key Stage 2 resources

Communication, Language and Literacy ed. Sally Gray, Scholastic (2006) (photocopiable activity sheets and CD-ROM)

Workabooks. The Primary School Homework Book Co Ltd, PO Box 49832, London NW5 1ZH Tel: 0845 1228623 Web: www.workabook.co.uk Series of six literacy work books covering Key Stages 1 and 2

Rainbow Readers – 26 books with 54 accompanying activities for children who are struggling to learn to read – www.ransom.co.uk

Boys Rule! and *Girls Rock!* series for SEN children published by Rising Stars – www.risingstars-uk.com

Developing Children's Non-Fiction Writing: working with writing frames by Maureen Lewis and David Wray, Scholastic (1996)

Getting the Buggers to Write by Sue Cowley, Continuum (2002)

101 Games for Social Skills by Jenny Mosley (and others), LDA (2003)

Circle Time: A practical book of Circle Time lesson plans by Jenny Mosley, Positive Press Ltd (2005)

Key Stage 3 resources

Key Stage 3 National Strategy *Early phonics for secondary pupils handbook*, DfES Ref: 0326/2002

Literacy in the Secondary School by Maureen Lewis and David Wray, David Fulton Publishers (2004)

Getting the Buggers to Write 2 by Sue Cowley, Continuum (2004)

Introducing Circle Time to Secondary Students by Charlie Smith, Lucky Duck (2003)

Useful contacts

National Literacy Trust, Swire House, 59 Buckingham Gate, London SW1E 6AJ Tel: 020 7828 2435 Web: www.literacytrust.org.uk

English Speaking Board (International) Ltd, 26a Princes Street, Southport PR8 1EQ Tel: 01704 501730 Web: www.esbuk.org